Dedication

For my wife, Rita Ititim-Aboh

About the Series

The African Humanities Series is a partnership between the African Humanities Program (AHP) of the American Council of Learned Societies and academic publishers NISC (Pty) Ltd. The Series covers topics in African histories, languages, literatures, philosophies, politics and cultures. Submissions are solicited from Fellows of the AHP, which is administered by the American Council of Learned Societies and financially supported by the Carnegie Corporation of New York.

The purpose of the AHP is to encourage and enable the production of new knowledge by Africans in the five countries designated by the Carnegie Corporation: Ghana, Nigeria, South Africa, Tanzania, and Uganda. AHP fellowships support one year's work free from teaching and other responsibilities to allow the Fellow to complete the project proposed. Eligibility for the fellowship in the five countries is by domicile, not nationality.

Book proposals are submitted to the AHP editorial board which manages the peer review process and selects manuscripts for publication by NISC. In some cases, the AHP board will commission a manuscript mentor to undertake substantive editing and to work with the author on refining the final manuscript.

The African Humanities Series aims to publish works of the highest quality that will foreground the best research being done by emerging scholars in the five Carnegie designated countries. The rigorous selection process before the fellowship award, as well as AHP editorial vetting of manuscripts, assures attention to quality. Books in the series are intended to speak to scholars in Africa as well as in other areas of the world.

The AHP is also committed to providing a copy of each publication in the series to university libraries in Africa.

AHP Editorial Board Members as at November 2018

AHP Series Editors:

Professor Adigun Agbaje, University of Ibadan, Nigeria
Professor Emeritus Fred Hendricks, Rhodes University, South Africa

Consultant:

Professor Emeritus Sandra Barnes, University of Pennsylvania, USA (Anthropology)

Published in this series

LANGUAGE AND THE CONSTRUCTION OF MULTIPLE IDENTITIES IN THE NIGERIAN NOVEL

ROMANUS ABOH

Publications

Published in South Africa on behalf of the African Humanities Program
by NISC (Pty) Ltd, PO Box 377, Grahamstown, 6140, South Africa
www.nisc.co.za

First edition, first impression 2018

ISBN: 978-1-920033-29-3 (print)

Manuscript mentor: Prof. Harry Garuba
Project manager: Peter Lague
Cover design: Advanced Design Group

Printed in South Africa by Digital Action

Contents

Acknowledgements

I acknowledge the postdoctoral fellowship support I have enjoyed from the African Humanities Program (AHP), which has offered me several opportunities to learn many things not only about academics, but about life in general. AHP's interest in supporting and giving budding African scholars the opportunity to advance their careers as well as strengthen African-humanities scholarship call for celebration.

I am particularly thankful to Professor Harry Garuba of Cape Town University, South Africa for critically reading this work. He proffered ideas that helped me to improve the quality of this work. I also wish to thank three people who taught me an immense amount about discourse analysis and pragmatics and how to engage discourses critically from an interdisciplinary perspective: Professors Tayo Lamidi, Obododimma Oha and Akin Odebunmi, all of the Department of English, University of Ibadan, Nigeria. In their respective ways, they contributed significantly to who I have become and what I know about discourse analysis, pragmatics and scholarship.

Professor Joseph Akawu Ushie of the Department of English, University of Uyo, Nigeria, has remained a significant part of my academic career and I am grateful to him. His private library provided the critical materials I depended on to lay the foundation for this book. In the course of writing, I also depended on his rich knowledge of Bette-Bendi cultural semantics. Our constant interactions on 'where stylistics and discourse analysis parted ways' further deepened my knowledge about the nexus of language and literature. Another academic who has been extremely supportive is Professor Luke Eyoh of the Department of English, University of Uyo. His kindness and geniality to younger scholars are greatly appreciated. I am also indebted to my colleagues in the Department of English, University of Uyo for the various ways they supported me during the writing of this book. I remember that when I was away at the University of Dar es Salaam, Dr Julia Udoudom assisted me in grading some of the scripts I could not grade.

In writing this book, I have depended on a platoon of friends with attending ears and urging minds: Happiness Uduk, Richard Akwagiobe, Isidore Adie, Eyoh Etim, Amaka Ezeife, Susan Okocha, Uche Oyali, Prince Wekpa, Charles Akinsete, Toja Okoh, and Mary Specht. Their friendship continues to water me like a tree planted by the riverside.

I am especially grateful to Nathan Suhr-Sytsma, a dear friend. Nathan has been very supportive. Since we met in 2010, Nathan and I have shared many ideas about scholarship and our regular conversations on postcolonial African literature have shaped the way I engage texts, encouraging me to take a more critical perspective. I also thank him so very much for writing this foreword. The contributions of two other people, Funke Oni who read Chapter 2 of this work in manuscript form and Ifeyinwa Okolo who read Chapter 5, enriched my understanding of the dynamic intersection of language and identity. To them I am grateful.

I am also grateful for the opportunity, over the years of writing this book, to have been able to present some of the chapters that make up this book at local and international conferences. I thank the conveners of these conferences for providing the platform from which I could share my ideas as well as learn from others, whose thoughts have helped to define this book in intriguing ways. Words alone cannot express my gratitude as I remember the enormous support I enjoyed from the Carnegie Fund for Conference Attendance (CFCA) of the Institute of International Education (IIE). Their grant enabled me to attend the Athens Institute for Education and Research Conference in 2016, where I presented the fifth chapter of this book.

Chapter 3 of this book was written when, in 2015, I was a fellow-in-residence at the University of Dar es Salaam, Tanzania where I met Mringe Chansa and Elijah Mwaifuge; they made my two-month stay memorable. Susan Kiguli, Benge Okot and Sylvester Kahyana, tenured faculties of the Department of Literature, Makerere University, Uganda, are great intellectuals I met at Makerere when I was a fellow-in-residence in 2017. I also met Haliima and Lillian – two library staff at Makerere Institute of Social Research who helped me in getting the books I needed at the library. I am grateful to them. It gives me joy to say thank you to Peter Lague. He was the copyeditor of this book. The book is readable because he edited it. Thank you, Barbara, AHP secretary at South Africa, for the fantastic intermediary role you play between AHP and fellows.

During the long period of preparing this book, I enjoyed the unconditional support of my family: Patrick Akande, your belief in me has been the spirit that has kept me going; Godwin Ukwu, your understanding has been the oil that has greased my fingers; Ashieta Aboh, Odey Aboh, Robinson Akande, John Ukwu and my mother, your sincere interest in my academic endeavour has been an inspiration.

My wife, Rita Ititim-Aboh, is one of my strongest pillars. Her consistent interest in this book was expressed in her concerns: 'Have you heard from AHP?'; 'What has Harry Garuba said?'; 'Has Nathan sent the foreword?', and so on. She remains the spine of my research endeavours. I have often had to be away, physically and emotionally; yet she has borne all these absences. While editing this book for submission to AHP Secretariat in South Africa, my wife and I were blessed with a little bundle of love, Beshi. She is the first fruit of our sublime love.

Professor Imoh Emenyi of the Department of English, University of Uyo, I thank you very much. The Gender Studies course I co-taught with you was very helpful; the course, under your mentorship, redefined my perspectives about gender intersections in the African context. Thank you too for always praying for me. My friend and brother in the Lord, Dr Imo Okon of the Department of English, University of Uyo, even in haste, I will not forget those moments of praying together and encouraging each other in the Lord. It is in the same vein that my gratitude knows no bounds as I remember the role my church, Rhema Missions International, a Core Kingdom Community of Congress WBN, played in my spiritual understanding of the world, of life as a journey to eternity. Rhema Missions has always emphasised handwork, humility and diligence.

Finally, I express my gratitude to Foresight Schools, Ikom, Cross River State, for the grants I received to attend conferences within Nigeria. Foresight Schools has been in the forefront of promoting academic excellence in Nigeria.

Foreword

In autumn 2016, novelist and publisher Eghosa Imaseun, in an article entitled 'A question of audience,' which appeared in The Guardian (Nigeria), gave Nigerian writers some advice, saying that they did themselves a disservice by explaining terms for readers outside Nigeria. 'To illustrate what I am trying to say,' he wrote, 'take this especially egregious instance from a book I thoroughly enjoyed, Sefi Atta's *Everything Good Will Come*: 'Sheri had prepared food I hardly saw in my father's house: *jollof* rice; *egusi* stew with crushed melon seeds, and *eba*, a meal made from ground cassava.' Although not noted by Imasuen, Atta herself had acknowledged her dissatisfaction with such explanatory tags in a 2011 interview with Elena Rodríguez Murphy in which she concluded that worrying too much about non-Nigerian readers 'weighs down your prose.' A couple weeks after Imasuen's piece appeared, however, another novelist, Chigozie Obioma, took aim at him in The Guardian (UK). For Obioma, Imasuen's complaint smacked of 'provincialism' or a deliberate attempt to limit one's audience. Obioma claimed not to limit his own audience to the people of Nigeria. As he put it, 'Why am I thinking in terms of national borders? Do I even believe they exist? [...] I believe that fiction, with its untrammelled nature, speaks to no one, and by so doing, speaks to all.' One might link this kind of universalism to Obioma's own biography: he took his degree at Cyprus International University before going on to study and work in the United States; his novel *The Fishermen* was shortlisted for the prestigious Man Booker Prize, based in London, and won a number of awards in the United States. The fact that he and his writing have crossed borders does not, however, negate the existence of borders. In 'A question of audience – redux,' Imasuen had the final word: 'But to attempt to write for all is to write for no one, is to sacrifice authenticity on the altar of a misunderstanding of the notion of universalism. Remember that the local is universal.' Imasuen practices what he preaches, as we can see from the opening line of his novel *Fine Boys*, published in Lagos in 2012: 'I remember something my father told me after I went with him on a visit to one *oyibo* oil executive.'

The book currently in your hands takes up the question of how Nigerian novels do things with words, to echo the title of J. L. Austin's lectures about performative language, including words like *jollof, egusi, eba* and *oyibo*. Its author, Dr. Romanus Aboh, inventively brings the fields of literature and sociolinguistics into contact with each other. Literary scholars too often focus *either* on the stylistic elements *or* on the political ideology of a text, but Dr. Aboh endeavours to show that literary language cannot be separated from the social uses to which it is put. He conceptualises literary writing and reading as a social rather than merely an aesthetic practice, a practice that is emplaced, as Imasuen suggests, in the local and the national, even if it can travel elsewhere. At the same time, Dr. Aboh introduces a new archive of language data into linguistics by analysing rich literary texts by the aforementioned Sefi Atta, as well as by Nigeria's most famous contemporary writer, Chimamanda Ngozi Adichie, and a comparatively unknown writer, Liwhu Betiang. Whether or not you are interested in Nigerian literature, this book provides a model of how to do critical discourse analysis with literary texts. Dr. Aboh is particularly interested in the construction and reconstruction of identities through language. His emphasis on the plural social identities of characters — and, indeed, novelists — provides an alternative to the tired opposition between individualist and collective modes of action. As a result, each chapter is organised around a different kind of identity — ethnic, cultural, national, and gender, respectively — and the language used to produce it.

For a literary scholar like myself, it is unusual to read chapters organised according to types of language work rather than a writer or literary work. This organisation affords Dr. Aboh the opportunity to point out striking parallels in how language is deployed across the selected novels and to delve into the intricacies of language use. The second chapter, on ethnic identity, focuses on naming practices as both essential to how ethnicity is constructed and revelatory of text as performance. Here the discussion of the dialectical relationship between characters' names and conduct is especially notable. The third chapter, on cultural identity, looks at novelists' employment of loanwords from Nigerian languages. In other words, why write 'eba' at all in an anglophone novel, rather than just 'a meal made from ground cassava'? Dr. Aboh contends that we can see literary work as a 'people's archive' upholding distinctive varieties of food, clothing, and dance as modes of cultural identity. The fourth chapter, on national identity, pays close attention to the invention of *Nigerianisms*, as well the selection of pronouns, to extend both Achebe's and Soyinka's classic rationale for Nigerianising literary English in order to account for language-in-use. Even as Nigerians question the future — and, at times, even the existence of their nation — they construct a national identity through everyday language choices. The fifth and final chapter takes up gender identity at a time when gender-based analysis is yielding some of the most exciting insights in African studies. It deals with the language of marriage and procreation, 'woman-women oppression' and the patriarchal subjection of women. Although I am not persuaded by that middle term — it seems to me that we should instead understand novelists like Adichie and Atta to be critiquing the extension of patriarchal oppression to women's relationships with each other — the chapter lays the ground for further attention and debate about the nexus of gender, language and power.

I met Romanus Aboh at the University of Ibadan in 2010, when we were both PhD candidates. I was immediately impressed with his intellectual drive and his determination to do high-quality work, not to mention his knowledge of contemporary writing. Having received his PhD in Discourse Analysis in 2013, Dr. Aboh is now mentoring the next generation of students and scholars. From a so-called minority language group himself, he is keenly attuned to how the politics of ethnic identification and language are intertwined in Nigeria. At the same time, his work is not so much a critique of majoritarian ethnic politics as an exploration of linguistic nuances founded on the conviction that literature can convey the vitality of real-life language. As he eloquently puts it in Chapter 3, 'people continually live in and through their language; they even die in it.' Unlike a strong version of the Sapir-Whorf hypothesis, according to which we are determined or even imprisoned by the conceptual tools of a given language, his book presents a hopeful view of the world, albeit one that acknowledges the possibility of conflict: through our interactions with each other, we are constantly creating new linguistic elements and thus remaking our own identities.

Nathan Suhr-Sytsma
Emory University, Atlanta, USA
April 2018

Preface

Writing and preparing this book, *Language and the Construction of Multiple Identities in the Nigerian Novel*, for publication took me about five years. This lengthy period was largely informed by the thorny nature of the subject of discourse — identity. The most difficult problem I had was how to structure the book into chapters in such a way that each chapter would discuss an identity type. So, I was at lost as to what to and what not to include in the book. My dilemma in dealing with the relationship between language and identity was further compounded by the heterogeneous nature of the data of my study — novels. In the course of trying to explore the interface of language and identity construction, I came to the realisation that the complex nature of my subject of discourse had to be approached from different perspectives. It needed to be viewed as you would watch a masquerade dancing in the playground: you have to move along with the masquerade as it dances round and round in order to quite appreciate its theatrics.

I therefore took an interdisciplinary approach (critical discourse analysis, literary discourse analysis and sociocultural analysis), drawing readers' attention to how the Nigerian novel provides compelling examples of the intersection of language deployed to construct identities in literary situations. In this respect, the Nigerian novel is overt in its pedagogical motive, namely to instruct its readers about Nigerian practices, beliefs, history and culture.

The textual and extra-textual analyses in this work examine a representation of Nigerian novels published between 2005 and 2013. The novelists concerned are described within the Nigerian critical paradigm as new voices, post-independence writers or third-generation writers, among other periodisation nomenclatures. However, my motive for the selection of their texts is informed by the texts' contemporaneity (even when the term contemporaneity has an expansive meaning) and because they are texts written by Nigerians which indicate a connection between the use of language and the construction and reconstruction of identities. I have combined both qualitative and quantitative analyses in this study. I am strongly motivated by the belief that a combination of these analytic approaches will bolster methods of doing discourse analysis.

Language and the Construction of Multiple Identities in the Nigerian Novel draws attention to the 'literariness' of discourse. The core of this book lies in portraying discourse analysis as a broad interdisciplinary field within linguistic enquiry. In so doing, the work is situated within literary discourse analysis. Locating this book within discourse analysis becomes expedient as it negates the unjustifiable assertion that any engagement with the language of literary texts falls within the purview of stylistics. The binding core of my argument, then, is that I do not see literature as *just* some aesthetic assemblage of linguistic lucidness or playfulness. In taking this position, I am furthering the literary discourse analysis postulate that meaning and language interface in multiple layers of language-in-use. In other words, the concept of art for art's sake does not quite apply to the Nigerian writer. Examining a writer's creative utilisation of the resources of language can be rewarding; however, it can be even more rewarding if we focus attention on the nuanced way language is deployed to construct and reconstruct identities.

List of Tables

1

Introduction

Beyond stylistic rhetoric

This study examines the interface of language and identity construction in the Nigerian novel. The African novel can be studied from various disciplines within the humanities because it challenges issues of subjectivity and experience in ways that are yet to be explored in academic-oriented exercises. Following largely the sociocultural dimension of literary discourse analysis, this book engages the Nigerian novel by focusing on the nexus between language and identity construction, arguing that the use of language in the construction of identity in literary discourse can reveal the multilayered interpretive discourse possibilities to which the 'language' of literature can be put (Porras 2011). This book examines questions of identities in selected Nigerian novels and attempts an alternative reading of the use of language with specific attention to the strategic and discursive enunciation of identities in the postcolonial Nigerian novel.

The preference for the Nigerian novel over other novels of African extraction is informed by two distinctly interrelated factors. First, the Nigerian novelist has been observed to have used the literary medium — which many non-Nigerian readers can easily access — as a means of projecting not only the Nigerian sociocultural experience, but also Nigerian identity as exemplified in the use of language. Second and closely related to the first is the widely accepted position that there is a Nigerian version of English, and this variety can be developed as a vibrant and productive medium of countering Western language globalisation (Jowitt 1991, Banjo 1996 and Eka 2000, among others). This consciousness, mediated through language, has influenced the way Nigerian authors utilise the English language, setting them apart from other African writers. The focus on the use of language in the Nigerian novel is simply informed by the fact that language and literature are related and are powerful vehicles for producing knowledge and identities.

The world over, writers have, through their artworks, shown that one of the overriding social functions of literature is the quest for identity construction, reconstruction and the enactment of ideologies. Eliot (1962) notes that the importance of any literary piece is not considered merely by its aesthetic quality, but also through the sociological germaneness of the work within the specific environment of its production. Following a similar analytic in an insightful essay entitled 'The Social Functions of the African Novel', Adebayo succinctly articulates the interface between literature and social reality in the African novel:

> The relationship between society and African literature in general and the novel in particular can be visualised along two lines: how literature has constituted itself into a model of analysis and synthesis of social reality, and the effect of literature on society. Since its beginnings, the primary role of the African novels has been to elucidate historical and social phenomena. (1987, 297)

So saying, Adebayo astutely details the relevance of literary works in the search for identity. Moreover, language plays an indispensable role in the production and reproduction of identities. This nexus between language and literature in terms of identity construction is worthy of scholarly engagement.

Despite flourishing critical works on language and identity construction in recent years, critics have paid scant attention to how language is deployed to create and negotiate identities in Nigerian novels. Much scholarship tends to focus on stylistic effects, neglecting the complexity and dynamism of the Nigerian novel which warrant linguistic discussion and multifaceted engagement. Relying on Fowler's theory of 'mind-style', for instance, Tunca (2014) undertakes a stylistic analysis of Chimamanda Adichie's *Purple Hibiscus*, concentrating on Kambili's use of language to facilitate a deeper understanding of how the thematic concepts of freedom and oppression are interlaced in the narrative structure of the novel.

In his article entitled 'Language and Style in Okot p'Bitek's *Songs of Ocol*', Salman (2013) submits that the success of Okot's poetic message is a result of carefully calibrated grammatical structures, particularly the clause structure. Salman's study centres on the interconnectedness between language and the presentation of a writer's creative initiative. This approach reminds one of how a writer's message confluences with the selected medium of articulation. Perhaps such conceptualisation makes Salman conclude his article by noting that 'stylistics is an interface between language and literature... This then means that a meaningful and worthwhile literary study should begin with the language used in the text' (2013, 124). Unmistakably enunciated in Salman's position is the idea that any study that deals with the language of African literature that is not entrenched within stylistic methodology or framework is 'meaningless and worthless'. This kind of position not only reduces the whole of linguistics to stylistics, but also closes off other possible linguistic approaches that can be applied in the reading and interpretation of the language of African literature. For

Aikoriogie to depend on lexical pragmatics in analysing 'pertinent morphological formations in Ngũgĩ wa Thiong'o's *Wizard of the Crow* and explain their significance' (2015, 34) in the context of the novel is a debunking of the fact that the analysis of literary language is only confined to stylistics.

Moreover, a critical examination of Okot's use of language can reveal how these syntactic fusions are structured to delineate the discourses of colonialism on one hand and cultural revival on the other. Expressed differently, it can be said that the 'nativisation' or 'aculturisation' of English, as evident in the transliteration strategy deployed by Okot, is, of course, not all about style, but about retaining the cultural reality of the Langi people of northern Uganda. In fact, a close engagement with Okot's use of language reveals his strategic deployment of language to change social order as well as shape identities. The use of phoric elements, for example, accounts for the poet's use of language to depict how asymmetrical power relations are discursively produced, sustained, negotiated and challenged in an African community.

It appears that it is not only Salman who holds the view that any 'meaningful and worthwhile' study of the language of Nigerian literature must be stylistic. Ayeleru (2011) has also endorsed this position. He argues that Nigerian novelists' adoption and adaptation of indigenous speech forms into the syntax of English is all about stylistic wordplay and interlanguaging. Ayeleru's position tends to undermine the constitutive role indigenous speech forms and language as a whole play in the construction of identity. Moreover, Ayeleru's view can hardly be differentiated from the general assumption in stylistics that '[t]he preferred object of study in stylistics is literature, whether that be institutionally sanctioned "Literature" as high art or more popular "canonical" forms of writing' (Simpson 2014, 3). Stylistics, invariably, only looks at the 'how' of language use without paying attention to the 'what' and 'why'.

The concern of stylistics with the language of literary texts does not suggest that any valid approach to the study of the 'language of literary texts' must take a stylistic path or be naturally stylistic in orientation. In fact, Achimbe has argued persuasively for a more dialectical conception of the use of language in the African context, in which he upholds the idea that 'borrowings from the indigenous languages into New Englishes are additive resources that facilitate the communicative needs within a community and should not, therefore, compromise the status [identity] of the speakers' (2013, 13). Accounting for the insufficiency of stylistics in providing deeper explication of literary texts, Bradford (1997, xi) insists, 'it [stylistics] must draw upon the terminology and methodology of disciplines which focus upon language in the real world'. Bradford suggests that in the real world our understanding of what words mean is quite often augmented by an infinite number of contextual and situational determinants — stylistics alone can hardly help us to understand the undercurrents of language-in-use.

Needless to say, many scholars have been misled to think that any engagement with the language of literature must be stylistic. In drawing attention to such a canonical fuss, Tunca cogently writes that the reason behind this 'misconception' is that:

> ...the aforementioned methodological limitations originate in scholars' disagreement, or even indecisiveness, over the source and methods of knowledge that should be used to carry out linguistic analyses of African literatures in English. Part of my argument is that these epistemological hurdles have presented themselves on at least two levels: that of the *origin* of the object of investigation, and that of the *discipline* of stylistics itself. (2014, 31–32)

Clearly instantiated in Tunca's view is the idea that the 'indecisiveness' suffered by critics of the language of African writings is informed by the matrix that any scholarly discourse with the 'object of investigation'— the African novel — must pay close attention to the aesthetic values of an artwork. But that is not the basic idea, for Tunca has also revealed that there are 'two distinct movements of linguistic research into African literatures: one focusing on the culturally-specific aspects of texts, and the other attempting a less context-dependent examination of literary pieces' (2014, 32). Obviously, linguistic research into the African novel, as argued earlier on, has focused primarily on aesthetic functionality, undermining the cultural significations that are embedded therein as manifest in writers' strategic use of language resources such as loaning, naming and Nigerianisms, among several other metadiscursive ways of using language to depict sociocultural initiatives. This book primarily follows the cultural approach, revealing that the language of the Nigerian novel, like other African novels, can be examined beyond its stylistic borders. Elaborating the abovementioned, Osundare reminds us that language and literature are important aspects of people's 'cultural and intellectual patrimony' (2012, 213). Ushie and Aboh (2014, 134) are also of the opinion that 'the study of Nigerian literature includes linguistic as well as historical, ethnological, sociocultural, and pedagogical approaches'. Yet, taking a culture-specific approach does not suggest disregarding the value of the artistic output of the Nigerian writer. To attempt to 'relegate the stylistic inventiveness of the Nigerian writer to the background', Ushie and Aboh (2014, 129) caution, is 'to reduce literature to polemics'. Sustaining Ushie and Aboh's position, Emmanuel and Aboh write: 'the linguistic nuances can become an interesting field of cultural studies' (2015, 140).

Using Liwhu Betiang's *The Cradle on the Scale* (2011), Chimamanda Ngozi Adichie's *Half of a Yellow Sun* (2007) and Sefi Atta's *A Bit of Difference* (2013) as representative Nigerian texts, and subjecting them to critical textual analysis, this book argues that the use of language in the Nigerian novel traverses stylistic wordplay to reflect how linguistic resources drawn from features of Nigerian English and other forms of language-in-use signal ethnic, cultural, national and gender identities in ideologically context-specific ways. It is hoped that examining the language of the Nigerian novel beyond its aesthetic functionality will provide critics of the language of Nigerian fiction with broader, deeper and alternative ways of examining literary discourse.

Establishing the canon

Having refuted the assumption that the use of language in the Nigerian novelistic discourse is all about stylistic nuances, this book illustrates the interconnectedness of language and identity construction by critically investigating what informs the peculiar ways Nigerian novelists use language in their literary compositions. For instance, when writers 'make' their fictional characters use specific loan words or certain speech forms, and assign specific names to them, it is not a mere stylistic practice. Rather, it is a deliberate act of identity construction since language is an identity building or formation material.

It is at such intersections that Adejunmobi sheds light on how an African writer's imaginative use of language is informed by the need to establish authentic African identity. In her words, there is 'an intimate correlation between the identity of literature and the language of its composition' (1999, 583–584). The following example taken from Okey Ndibe's *Arrows of Rain* substantiates this argument:

> She is an *ogbanje*. Only an *ogbanje* would smile at death. I am certain of that. *Ogbanje*. They can die and return to life over and over again. To them, death is a game, that's why they can laugh at it. Death only means a brief visit to the land of spirits. Then they return to life. (2000, 8)

It is interesting to see how Ndibe adopts *ogbanje* from his Igbo language to describe spirit-children who complete the circle of birth, death and rebirth by the same mother. In Yoruba cosmology, such children are referred to as *abiku*. The excerpt clearly shows that the motivation for the use of the Igbo expression is neither for its stylistic significance nor to fill up some narrative space, but a conscious linguistic exercise aimed at bringing to the novelist's readers' attention a worldview, the way of life of the Nigerian people, specifically the Igbo. This is a practical cultural retention. The adoption and adaptation of indigenous linguistic expressions then are testimonies to the fact that the Nigerian novelist, though continuing to write in English, uses English in such a way that it heaves with sociocultural as well as nationalistic thoughts. It is necessary to note that *ogbanje/abiku* is a recurring phenomenon in Nigerian literature. If it is persistent, we then need to ask *why* do Nigerian writers keep bringing up this phenomenon rather than quickly conclude that it is all about style. Perhaps the frontiers of our knowledge of language-in-use will be expanded beyond the horizon of stylistics if we look keenly at the fact that, in postcolonial societies, identity construction is better understood in the way language is used in literary situations.

Scholars have pointed out that literature recreates the real world of a people. The implication is that if the use of language in the Nigerian novel is interpreted outside the magnified context of identity construction, the real picture of existence and co-existence in Nigeria will be blurred. The Nigerian novelists' recourse to the 'nativisation' of the English language is not a mere stylistic practice or choice, but is aimed at expanding the frontiers of English to accommodate their worldview — hence identity.

In conjunction with the abovementioned, while some scholars have considered code alternation and transliteration as the result of a lack of linguistic facility by African writers in expressing some indigenous concepts, it is important to stress here that this is not the case, but is instead because they are conscious of the fact that their language displays their identity (Aboh 2012b). Okunrinmeta's position that Nigerian writers use language 'to tap their bilingual experiences to adapt the languages at their disposal to suit the numerous conveniences, experiences, nuances and sensibilities in the Nigerian environment' (2013, 117) deflates the idea that code-switching/mixing, as argued by Bandia (1996), is evidence of the absence of linguistic facility. So saying, Okunrinmeta elucidates Achebe's (1975) idea that the African writer has to calculatingly 'make' English bear the burden of his or her dynamic and complex experiences. Therefore, Nigerian novelists, through the use of language, succeed in expressing their bilingual identity. The use, then, of indigenous expressions in the Nigerian novel captures nuances of new sensibilities emerging and re-emerging from history, politics and the sociocultural life of the Nigerian people. The insistence of this study is that the relationship between the use of language in the Nigerian novel and cultural consciousness is mutually reinforcing and explains how cultural, ethnic, gender and national awareness act on language use and how the use of language also shapes identity, capturing in an inexplicable yet interesting manner the ambivalence of the Nigerian linguistic reality. Undoubtedly, stylistics cannot answer some storied fundamental questions of human existence which are reflected in the sampled Nigerian novels. The critical point here is not to devalue stylistics but to draw attention to the fact that the interfaced bond between a writer's imaginative use of language and identity construction is not merely a matter of style.

Elucidating the foregoing position, Hall argues that writers who are conscious of the problematics of identities do not 'select' their words haphazardly, but 'write and speak from a particular place and time, from a history and a culture which is specific' (2013, 222). We would, perhaps, agree that what an individual writer does is to expand the borders of language, so as to accommodate as well as express the social needs of a people and their cultural orientation or realities. To treat language therefore as an individual's 'commodity', as conceived in certain stylistic circles (see Bradford 1997), is not only unprogressive, but blurs how individual writers exploit the resources of language to give expressive force to sociocultural realities. Fictional writers, specifically Nigerian novelists, use language to create fictional worlds, which reconstruct the real Nigerian world. The point being stressed here is that a reading of the Nigerian novel beyond stylistic conventions will provoke a deeper and more holistic understanding of how Nigerian novelists work out meaning through linguistic calibration.

In combination with the aforesaid, it is necessary to state that Nigerian novelists use indigenous expressions from Nigerian languages to reflect the many languages as well as subcultures in Nigeria. Some Yoruba examples gleaned from Liwhu Betiang's *The Cradle on the Scale* suffice for now:

> The crown-witness told how Andoukeye had boiled and eaten yam in the afternoon after preparing *eba* for them to eat; ... (2011, 10)

> They surrounded him, touching and admiring him as they scrambled to take his *amebo* paper-bag from right and left. (2011, 78)

Although the various contextualised and situationalised significations of loanwords shall later be accounted for, it is expedient to highlight here that the italicised loanwords are drawn from the Yoruba language, one of the largest ethnic groups in Nigeria. While *eba* describes paste made from processed cassava, *amebo* is a Yoruba word for gossip, depending on the context in which the word is used. Such linguistic representations produce novels with multicultural and multilingual backgrounds which are, by and large, representative of the multicultural system of the Nigerian nation. Anyokwu, to a large extent, supports this assertion as he writes that 'Nigeria being a multilingual and multi-ethnic country with English as the official language, the phenomenon of inter-language and syntactic fusion is very prevalent' (2011, 83). What follows therefore is the production of literature that speaks on behalf of the multi-ethnic nationalities that make up the geopolitical entity called Nigeria.

Even though Betiang, the author of *The Cradle on the Scale*, is not Yoruba, but a Bette-Bendi person — one of the smallest groups of people and language spoken in Obudu, northern Cross River State— the loaning of Yoruba expressions typifies the linguistic situation in Nigeria. Betiang does not speak Yoruba but understands and uses a few words with Yoruba ancestry in his creative writing. In fact, this is where the selection of recently published Nigerian novels both from 'small' and 'large' ethnic groups is important, especially in the interrogation of the connection between language and identity construction. The reader of the Nigerian novel published at the turn of the twenty-first century must attempt to re-negotiate the cultural meaning of new ethnic relationships against a myriad of pre-existing ideas about ethnic and cultural affinity or belonging, or even unbelonging. In fact, the reader may want to ask why Betiang prefers Yoruba expressions to Igbo ones, one of the main spoken languages in the southeast of Nigeria from where he comes. This lexical strategy, in the first instance, demonstrates Betiang's affiliation with Yoruba as an ethnic group; in the second instance, it reveals that the 'new' Nigerian is aware of the multiple languages and cultures that are in Nigeria and their writings not only capture the multilingual situation, but promote the peaceful existence of multilingual/multi-ethnic Nigeria. Such a desire for pluralism produces novels with multicultural and multi-ethnic backgrounds which are representative of Nigeria's multi-ethnic reality. This positioning is not too far to seek. As simplistic as this may appear, the use of language in the earlier works of prominent pioneer Nigerian novelists — Chinua Achebe (*Things Fall Apart* and *Arrow of God*), Wole Soyinka (*The Interpreters*) and Elechi Amadi (*The Concubine*), among others — does not suggest that they promote a multilingual and multicultural Nigeria. This is manifest in the fact that they borrowed, code-mixed and code-switched, among other linguistic acts only from their indigenous languages. Although this cannot be said of Achebe's *Anthills of the Savanah*, it is obvious that these writers were merely looking 'inward', mostly concerned about where they come from rather than the country they belong to. In her book, *Bearing Witness: Readers, Writers and the Novel in Nigeria*, Griswold upholds the view that some early Nigerian novels show how their 'authors are determined to perpetuate and enhance their native languages' (2000, 31). While this cannot be said of Cyprian Ekwensi's *People of the City* (because the characterisation and use of language indicate a typical multilingual/multicultural Nigeria), much of this seemingly 'ethnic writing' can be thought of in Achebe's first and third novels. The use of language in the novel appears as though the author had never met Nigerians or interacted with Nigerians from other ethnic groups. The truth is that the novels were written specifically about the Igbo of southeastern Nigeria.

The preceding argument indicates that the sampled writers' use of language demonstrates a preference for an ethnically and culturally diverse nation — the motivation for preferring them over other Nigerian novelists. It allows Nigerians to retain their ethnic identity alongside national identity. In fact, this is where the adoption of the socio-ethno-linguistic theory (as one of the theoretical foundations) to the analysis of ethnic, cultural and national identities is significant to the explication of literature as social discourse. Oyeleye, elaborating the views of Fowler (1981), lends credence to this as he writes that literature is social discourse since it is in different ways 'defined and controlled by social institutions within which it is embedded' (1991, 89). To have an in-depth understanding of the use of language in the Nigerian novel, there is need for the analyst to bear in mind the 'social-linguistic' situation in

Nigeria. The present challenge for Nigeria, as can be inferred from the sampled texts, is how to embrace diversity while simultaneously privileging ethnic sentiments. It is a challenge worth investigating, considering the complex and dynamic linguistic strategies employed in the Nigerian novel published in the twenty-first century. The intellectual class is conscious of this ambivalence. The novels selected for this book are therefore analysed in relation to how they reflect the idea of multiple, competing cultures (ethnic groups) and gender asymmetries in Nigeria, as well as the need to uphold a national identity.

The purposeful selection of the novels is informed by how the sampled works navigate the seams of the personal through cross-cultural realities to the political use of language in relation to the construction and negotiation of identities. It is therefore hoped that the carefully selected texts will serve as representative texts even when there are slight variations both in the way they use language and in their thematic thrust. Be that as it may, a critical engagement with the selected texts will indicate that post-independence Nigerian novels share many commonalities — Nigeria's postcolonial and literary histories, for example, interweave in remarkably defining shades. Similarly, novels are preferred to other literary forms because they offer both scholars and students of African culture insights into how language depicts arguments and counter-arguments on identities and the politics of existence. These ideas make the Nigerian novel a critical tool for economic, political, historical and, importantly, cultural studies. The notion that diverse ideas are thematised in the Nigerian novel draws symbolically from Ngugi's (1997) thoughts that literature is never written in a vacuum. Thus, the Nigerian novel, as an art form, provides exquisite examples of political, economic, social and cultural ideologies and identities which completely resonate with the realities of the Nigerian people.

Identity as a linguistic phenomenon

Identity has been widely studied from the viewpoints of cultural anthropology and social psychology, and it seems superfluous to dwell on what other scholars have already exposed. Linguists who are interested in identity discourse have borrowed methods extensively from the abovementioned disciplines in their interrogation of the nexus between language and identity (Windt-Val 2012; Kroskrity 1999; Hristova 2014). Identity is a linguistic phenomenon because people use language as a vehicle to instantiate their identity, their belonging and unbelonging to certain social categories — sex, ethnic, cultural, national. The formulation and reformulation of an identity, whether consciously or unconsciously, is largely calibrated through language. It is relevant to point out here that the way a writer uses language has to do with the search for identity, for the discovery of self. Since identity is pervasive, it is often carried through the medium of language. Even our dress style that says something about us is quite often accounted for through the name we assign to it.

Although there are multiple descriptions of the notion of identity in the literature on identity discourse, the majority of scholars are agreed that identity is understood 'in terms of who the people are to each other and how different kinds of identities are produced in spoken interaction and written discourse' (Benwell and Stokoe 2006, 6). In an attempt to simplify the complex dynamics of identity in order to bring about 'a reasonable degree of cohesion', Omoniyi and White (2006, 2) present a common position taken by identity scholars:

1   that identity is not fixed;
2   that identity is constructed within established contexts and may vary from one context to another;
3   that these contexts are moderated and defined by intervening social variables and expressed through language(s);
4   that identity is a silent factor in every communicative context whether given prominence or not;
5   that identity informs social relationships and therefore also informs the communicative exchanges that characterise them;
6   that more than one identity may be articulated in a given context in which case there will be a dynamic of identities management.

Omoniyi and White's summary puts forward the idea that identity is best approached when multiple linguistic methods and theories are utilised. Language plays a central role in both interpreting and enacting identity (Joseph 2004). Language is a critical component in the construction of identity (Clarke 2007). Although language is not identity, it gives expression to identity (Aboh 2012b). The fact is that language holds the key to understanding people's relation to social events and offers insights into the expression of reality. The conjecture is that the concept of identity can hardly be adequately discussed without a detailed analysis of language in social practice. The centrality of the abovementioned position is that the way identity is negotiated or constructed is connected with the belief systems of the language user in relation to happenings in society. This functional way of looking at the use of language enables the analyst to know what language is 'saying' or 'not saying', 'doing' or failing to 'do'. This understanding of the way language functions suggests a distinctively inseparable link between language and identity.

The system of naming or names is an example of how identity is a matter of language. Joseph strongly posits, 'the entire phenomenon of identity can be understood as a linguistic one' (2004, 12). Beyond the use of names in establishing linguistic identity, there is the manifestation of personality, i.e. either as an individual or as a member of a group. This is a form of social identity where individuals employ linguistic items to identify with the people they consider theirs or members of their group. In this regard, language is a constant of identity with which people surround themselves according to their linguistic identity (Paltridge 2006; Cameron 2001). The tendency for people to associate freely with other people is always facilitated by the fact that the people involved speak the 'same' language. This line of reasoning indicates that identity is a reflection of people's individuality, and language either helps individuals in constructing respective forms of identities or hinders them from doing so. Le Page explains how identity is a linguistic phenomenon:

> People create their linguistic system and we all have more than one so as to resemble those of the group with which from time to time they wish to identify. Both the groups and their linguistic attributes exist solely in the mind of each individual…We behave in the way that — unconsciously or consciously — we think appropriate to the group with which at moment we wish to identify. (1986, 23)

Linguistic identity, Le Page's position suggests, is not an inescapable fate imposed on us, but to some extent at least, as social construct, a matter of choice. These identity constructions become particularly significant in a multilingual country like Nigeria with over 400 languages. In the sampled novels, each novelist is found to draw cultural and linguistic insights from their respective languages as a way of demonstrating their ethnic origin and of fostering their cultural and national identities.

Language plays a significant role in the formation of identity. Calvet (1997) affirms that to speak a language or a language form, to prefer the use of one form rather than another or to pretend to use one form rather than another is always something more than simply using an instrument of communication. Such a line of reasoning implies that speaking a language always indicates something besides what one is saying in the language. When, for instance, two lecturers in a department of English speak English to each other, although they have the same mother tongue (such as Bette-Bendi), their choice of English over Bette-Bendi should not be taken for granted. They connote the desire to conform to an international model; and in so doing, they encode their difference from others: the fact that they have studied, that they have university degrees, that they identify with the system that educated them and that they desire that the training they have received should form the operational foundation of the department. If in the same department, lecturers with the same background as the others express themselves in their mother tongue, the lecturers in question connote rejection, both of the colonial language and of belonging to it.

It must however be noted that language closeness does not necessarily guarantee social or ideological closeness. Small differences can become hugely significant from an ideological angle. However, these ways of referring to language as markers of identity are felt to resist unwarranted and dangerous assumptions of ethnic purity. Once people stand in ideological opposition, it seems a difficult task for language to bring them together.

Theoretical approaches

This study adopts socio-ethno-linguistic analysis, critical discourse analysis and literary discourse analysis as its theoretical points of reference in the analysis of the interaction of language and identity as reflected in the Nigerian novel. While the socio-ethno-linguistic analysis will account for language and identity and the nuanced ways language is deployed to reflect sociocultural identities, there is need to blend it with approaches that will provide fertile grounds for understanding the literariness of identity discourse as well as the social and political instances to which language is put.

Socio-ethno-linguistic analysis

Two basic approaches have been employed in the discourse of identity: essentialism and social constructionism. A close scrutiny of these two approaches reveals that neither is adequate on its own. Scholars such as Joseph (2004) and Porras (2011) have advocated a synthesis of the two approaches, rather than promoting one over the other, because it is more robust than anyone-sided approach. The need to follow an approach that accounts for the glaring inadequacies of both methods becomes imperative: socio-ethno-linguistic analysis.

Aboh (2014a) is not the only scholar who has adopted the socio-ethno-linguistic approach in analysing the language-identity nexus. Joseph (2004, 90) illustrated that essentialism cannot be entirely eschewed in identity discourse because 'constructing an identity is in fact constructing an essence'. He goes on to argue that 'the analyst who refuses any truck with essentialism risks missing a factor of the highest importance in the identity's construction'. For Blommaert (2005), essentialised identity is not different from socially constructing identity, or the conceptualisation of identity 'as a form of socially meaningful practice' that can as a matter of fact be 'seen as one particular form of performing identity' (2005, 208). Drawing attention to the thin line of demarcation between these two approaches to identity discourse, Blommaert perceptibly argues:

> Essentialising inscriptive statements on the 'quality' of students, for instance, are the prerogative of faculty, and a discourse on how good or bad students are this semester is a particular, powerful enactment of *inhabited* professorial group identity — *performing* specific forms of 'othering' is an ingredient of many forms of identity performance. (2005, 208; emphasis added)

Two key items in the above position should interest us: *inhabited* and *performing*. While 'inhabited' symbolises the primordial desire of a group, 'performing' describes the social constructedness of identity. The implication is that, although identity is socially constructed, it has some alignment with a given core — an essence. Put differently, conceiving identity as a social practice requires appreciating and working on essentially given facts — as an operational foundation or a take-off point. Socio-ethno-linguistic analysis embraces the essentialist's approach which perceives identity as a frame in which individuals identify either consciously or unconsciously with those with whom they feel a common bond because of similar traditions, behaviour, values and beliefs. Theorists of socio-ethno-linguistic analysis treat identity 'as a socially constructed category: it is whatever people agree it to be in any given historical and cultural context' (Benwell and Stockoe 2006, 9). Socio-ethno-linguistic analysis, besides considering identity as given, investigates how people perform, negotiate, construct and reconstruct identities. Theorists of this persuasion are particularly concerned about 'how it means to "have an identity" is produced in talk and text of all kinds' (Benwell and Stockoe 2006, 10). The implication is that while we look at identity through the prisms of the given and the constructed, our focus should also be on how language is used in context-specific ways to account for identity construction.

Porras (2011) has demonstrated how a socio-ethno-linguistic approach reflects the interchange of intrinsic structural processes used in terms of linguistic variation as well as extrinsic sociocultural factors such as race, ethnic identity, and social stereotypes. Porras's (2011) adoption of the socio-ethno-linguistic theory in the analysis of language in poetry reveals how linguistic membership or demonstrating affinity to an ethnic group can be calibrated through language and by certain cultural aspects that are peculiar to an ethnic group. In this way, Porras emphasises the role language and culture play in constructing not only ethnic identity, but also a national identity. A socio-ethno-linguistic framework enables us to approach ethnic, cultural, gendered and national identities through the analysis of linguistic items deployed by writers or, more precisely, by their literary characters. Ethnic, cultural, gender and national identities are discourse events that continue to emerge and are negotiated and constructed based on different linguistic resources and contexts. Therefore, the socio-ethno-linguistic approach, which assumes an intrinsic emotional connection between individuals and their language, is employed in this work to cater for the linguistic as well as the social constructedness of ethnic, cultural, gender and national identities in the selected novels. This book, by critically engaging the selected writers' discourse acts, will provoke a better understanding of how individuals and groups construct and project images of themselves that are not independent of and do not pre-exist the social contexts in which they are displayed and negotiated. Arguing in favour of a blend of the essentialism and social constructionist approaches in relation to ethnic identity construction, Ushie and Aboh (2013, 40) maintain:

> Though socially negotiated, ethnic demarcation lines are essentially existent in the sense that they form an important core of people's sociolinguistic realities, while ethnicity itself is not primordial, it is often viewed as such by individuals who lay claim to an ethnic identity.

The above summation implies the conceptualisation of ethnic or national identity as a social construct or practice that derives from extant essential cultural values that are unique to a group as well as distinguishes them from other groups. We can neither take as irrelevant membership in social categories such as ethnicity, class, or gender nor conjecture the aspects of social practices that are relevant for the explication of those essential categories.

Along similar lines, Aboh (2014a) maintains that since identity construction persists in the wider society because of cultural heritage, and situational and circumstantial experiences, it is important therefore for any theory or empirical investigation of identity enactment to take into account not only the social constructionist perspective in the pursuit of social interest, but the linguistic as well as the cultural formulation and the shared sense of descent that individuals derive from the essential core of their existence. The implication of following a socio-ethno-linguistic approach in this study means that the investigation of ethno-cultural and national identities construction in the sampled Nigerian novels is based on, first, the identification of the formal linguistic features (names, loanwords, pronominalisation, etc.) that are deployed by the sampled novelists; and, second, by the social contextual meanings with which they are imbued. Examining the linguistic features of the selected texts will reveal the crucial involvement of language in the construction of identity in the Nigerian novel and identity discourse as an outcome of society's communicative transactions. This symbolic relation between language and society calls for a critical engagement with the texts; hence, the need for critical discourse analysis.

Critical discourse analysis

Discourse, in the first instance, has to be critical in its analysis of texts because discourse analysts agree that often concealed in discourses are layers of significations that inform what is said; why and how it ought to be said; what is not said and why and how it is not said. The term 'critical' connotes 'critique' (Weiss and Wodak 2003, 14) in that it details the core concern of critical discourse analysis in 'revealing', bringing 'awareness', and the 'ideological functions of language in producing, reproducing or changing social structures, relations and identities' (Mayr 2004, 5). This 'awareness raising' approach to discourse is quite useful for the analysis of the Nigerian novel not only 'because it relates literature to particular world views, through a detailed study of the practices and choices of language, but also provides discourse analysis with the means of critically reading works of literature' (Ushie and Aboh 2014, 133).In other words, the overall social nature of literary texts — both the linguistic (micro) and extra-linguistic (macro) — which the sampled novelists deploy to enact their ideological positions and construction of identities can be understood better when we take a critical path.

Current studies within discourse analysis have seen discourse analysts tilting towards a critical analytical orientation. The goal of critical discourse analysis practitioners is to 'describe how language works in order to understand it, just as the physicist is to describe how the physical world works in order to understand it' (Gee 2005, 9). Popularly referred to as critical discourse analysis, and often abbreviated as CDA, the contribution of critical language analysis to language analysis lies in its strength for a broad, diverse, multidisciplinary and problem-oriented programme that can select its methods and areas of analysis on the basis of a theoretical analysis of social issues (van Dijk 2001; Fairclough 2001;Wodak 2010).In this way, CDA 'conceives discourse as a social phenomenon and seeks, consequently, to improve the social-theoretical foundations for practicing discourse analysis as well as for situating discourse in society' (Blommaert 2005, 27).CDA therefore connects a text to its wider social context.

Since it is the literary text that is being considered, with its diverse linguistic resonances and varied exploration of linguistic artefacts indicative of how ways of using language and doing things determine literary production, it is apt to work with a method that takes a critical approach to language analysis. It is critical in the sense that it shows connections and causes that are hidden people's strategic way of using language. It also implies intervention such as providing resources for those who may be disadvantaged through change. The exposure of hidden things is very important as they are not obvious for the people involved and therefore cannot be challenged. A critical approach to discourse therefore seeks to link the linguistic features (micro-level) with the underlying power structure (macro-sociocultural practice level) through discourse practices from which the text was drawn (meso-level) (McGregor 2003). Consequently, a text, a description of something that is happening in a larger social context replete with a complex set of power relations, is interpreted and acted upon by readers or listeners, depending on their rules, norms and mental models of socially acceptable behaviour. Oppression, repression and marginalisation go unchallenged if the text is not critically examined to reveal power relations and dominance.

CDA researchers focus on how social relations, identity, knowledge and power are constructed through written and spoken texts. From this critical perspective, discourse always involves power and how ideologies are connected to the past and current contexts interpreted differently by different people given their various backgrounds. The fact is that discourse and language can be used to create unequal power relations and portrayals of social groups that appear to be common sense, normal and natural when in reality they are not so. Using just words, those in power or wishing to be so, can influence the way we view things. The text is a record of an event where something is communicated. That is, it involves the presentation of facts and beliefs, the construction of identities of the participants discussed in the communication and strategies to frame the content of the message.

These strategies, in what Fairclough (1995, 2001) calls 'discourse practice', refer to the ways the dominant class manipulates language to present social issues as though they are beneficial to the consumers of text. They are the 'unspoken spoken rules' (absences) and conventions that govern how individuals learn to think, act and speak in all the social positions they occupy in life. Discursive practices involve ways of being in the world that signify specific and reasonable social identities. The text, which is situated in a social context (classroom, family, market, conference, campaign ground, etc.), becomes more than just use of words; it discloses the conventions which guide the use of such words.

Despite the fact that CDA mediates between the social and the linguistic and 'theorise[s] the social as more than mere contextual "backdrop" or "determiner" of text' (Benwell and Stokoe 2006, 105), it has been variously criticised for being too 'political' in its approach to language as well as lacking a single or unified method for analysing discourse. In response to this critique, two points can be made in favour of CDA. First, language itself is a political process: there is nothing wrong for the discourse analyst employing the methods of CDA to bring out the political content of texts. In fact, the choice of one language, in the case of a bilingual, or the choice of one language over another in a multilingual communicative situation by a language user is a political process in itself. The language user would have gauged the situation before making the choice. Second, the absence of defined analytical method(s) and the range of approaches is 'emblematic of the eclecticism and pluralism of the term "critical discourse analysis" itself' (Benwell and Stokoe 2006, 105).

Micro-level analysis deals with the properties of language. It looks at the meaning of formal linguistic features such as morphology, lexis, syntax, semantics and so on and functional ones such as sociolinguistics, pragmatics, etc. Scholars of CDA hold the view that there are strong and pervasive connections between linguistic structure and social structure, claiming that discourse cannot exist without social meanings (Wodak 2006). The discourse-historical approach that is followed in this study implies that the investigation of the construction of ethno-cultural and national identities in the sampled Nigerian novels is based on first, the identification of the formal linguistic features that are deployed by the sampled novelists and, second, by the social contextual meanings they are imbued with from the historical dimension. Examining the linguistic features of the selected texts will reveal, in an explicit manner, the crucial involvement of language in the construction of identity in the Nigerian novel and identity discourse as an outcome of events in society.

Working against the backdrop of linguists' claim that 'linguistic structure is not arbitrary, but is determined by, or motivated by the functions it performs' (Fowler 1981, 28), the analysis of the language of the texts relies on the social and personal needs they are detailed to perform by the novelists as well as the discourse participants. In relation to the context in which a word or sentence is used, it can have some significance assigned to it. The novel is a linguistically constructed system of beliefs, identities, ideologies and so on, which usually critically demonstrates a relationship between the text producer and the historical conditions that determined the production of the text (Yahya 2003). The critical analyst therefore must bear in mind that the linguistic choices that are made carry socially interpretable meanings and the analysis of language should rely on the historical contexts of the text composer at production stage with the understanding of the sociocultural nature of meaning. It is axiomatic that writers produce their texts from a particularly determined ideological perspective, as no text is completely neutral or value-free (Simpson 1993). Writers' universes are manifest in their discourse practices through concepts, discourse strategies and linguistic clues which allow them to reconstruct their personal ideological viewpoints in relation to particular events in society. In the recreation of experiences, a complex interplay of ethnic, national and cultural identities is at work, woven with the writer's ideological affiliations, which are constructed on the lines of the historical experiences that are recreated.

The macro-level analysis emphasises historical, contextual and interpretive analysis. It advocates innovative and evaluative analysis of texts beyond the horizons of language. The analysis of language from a social perspective works in harmony with Wodak's position that a critical analysis of a text should depend on 'specific historical traditions and socio-political contexts of the speakers and discourse' (2006, 15). The application of this sociological approach to text analysis enables analysts to identify the innovative ways language is used to construct users' ideological positions, power interplay and identity thereby accounting for the 'silences' that are hidden in texts. The macro-level analysis reveals an intertwined bond among formal linguistic features, the intended meaning, the communicative goal and society (Joseph 2004). The data under consideration reveal the ascription that discourse is a social process and social practice that can be used to accomplish interesting social goals.

Literary discourse analysis

Fowler explains that:

> [To] treat literature as discourse is to see the text as mediating relationships between language-users: not only relationships of speech, but also of consciousness, ideology, role and class. The text ceases to be an object and becomes an action or process. (1981, 80)

The notion of literature as discourse and, in particular the *literariness* of discourse, has been taken up by scholars such as Verdonk (2002), Widdowson (1975), Short (1998), Thornborrow and Wareing (1998) and Maingueneau (2010), among other literary discourse analysts. Verdonk (2002), for example, contends that since literature, like language, captures an interaction between people and between institutions and people, a study that recognises this perspective should therefore stress its interpersonal dimensions, and concentrate on those parts of textual structures which reflect and influence relations within discourse.

Maingueneau (2010, 147) insightfully argues that literary discourse analysis is about 'analysis' because it 'considers the reciprocal environment of text and context, which implies shifting the core of the analysis: from the creator and his other work to the conditions that make literary discourse possible'. The implication of following this trend of argument is that rather than see literature as a merely aesthetic medium, literature is best conceptualised as social. It follows that the discourse analysts hardly dwell on the aesthetics of literary texts, as their focus is on the political contents or discourses of texts. This suggests that what a writer does with the systems or resources of language is inseparable from the social events and conditions which shape its production. A further explanation gleaned from Adichie's *Half of a Yellow Sun* is quite helpful:

> Kainene snorted, 'Socialism would never work for the Igbo!' She held the brush suspended in mid-air. 'Ogbenyealu is a common name for girls and you know what it means? "Not to Be Married by a Poor Man." To stamp that on a child at birth is capitalism at its best'. (2007, 91)

Although Chapter 2 interrogates the bond of language and ethnic identity construction, especially through the use of names, it is imperative to quickly note that Kainene's linguistic construction demonstrates how events in society determine what a writer includes or excludes in his or her artwork. The fragment above illustrates literature's exploitation of the resources of language in creating and recreating discourses, in projecting a people's ethnic identity as well as an economic ideology. Besides the fact that Kainene relies on her Igbo cultural values to polemically resist the imposition of a politico-economic ideology that does not align with the economic reality of the Igbo, Kainene's deployment of the Igbo name — Ogbenyealu — is a deliberate act of Igbo ethnic identity construction — a symbolic explication of the literariness of discourse.

Fowler, cited earlier, writes of how literature as discourse is inevitably answerable and responsible; it cannot be 'cocooned from an integral and mobile relationship with society by evasive critics' strategies such as "implied author", "persona", "fiction";' (1981, 94) and so on. It is not as though these principles do not apply; the fact is that literature, seen as discourse, goes way beyond such principles to account for linguistic systems that, to a reasonable degree, reveal ideological undercurrents or sentiments. In this way, literature is an explication of discourses because when writers create, they use the resources of language available to them in such a manner that they reflect society's needs as well as how these affect writers' linguistic calibration of ideas. The reflexivity between linguistic choices and discourses tells us that '[t] he particular form taken by the grammatical system of language is closely related to the social and personal needs that language is required to serve' (Halliday 1970, 142). Literature becomes discourse as it makes language more socially relevant. This is because literature derives from the social and economic discourses of particular societies. Literature then is discourse, i.e. 'an open set of texts, of great formal diversity, recognised by a culture as posing certain constitutional values and performing certain functions' (Fowler 1981, 81).

Literature's role as a medium of self-discovery is a well-established position in scholarship. The example below, taken from Sefi Atta's *A Bit of Difference*, explains this as Deola at an American airport observes how the use of some expressions signal self-discovery:

> It takes her a while to get her luggage and she ends up behind a Nigerian woman whose luggage is singled out for an X-ray before hers is.
> 'Any *garri* or *egusi*?' a custom official asks the woman playfully.
> 'No,' the woman replies, tucking her chin in, as if she is impressed by his pronunciation.
> '*Odabo*,' the customs officer says and she waves after he inspects her luggage.
> The woman waves back. The camaraderie between them is tantamount to exchanging high fives… (Atta 2013, 2)

The first thing that may interest a reader of the above excerpt is the *singling* out of the Nigerian woman *for X-ray*. Does this capture the kind of ill-treatment some Nigerians suffer at international gates? Second, there is an explicit construction of a Nigerian cultural identity as evident in the loanwords *odabo, garri* and *egusi*. This calculated use of language conduces an air of camaraderie between the woman and the customs official (though not Nigerian) as they exchange high fives. (This is discussed in Chapter 3 in greater detail. The effort here is to lay a foundation for the kind of discussion we encounter later in the book). But then, the discourse analyst will ask questions such as, *why* does the novelist deploy such expressions? What is the undercurrent for using such expressions? How do language users rely on the linguistic resources available to them in the situation they find themselves in to achieve their desired social goals? This discursive practice indicates that in a literary discourse situation, literature ceases to be a mere object and transforms to an action or process. While this perspective appears to be 'anti-formalist', there is however the willingness of literary texts to be 'kinetic'. A text, then, is an explication of social processes, the communicative interaction of implied speakers and thus of consciousness and of communities (Fowler 1981, 94). Central to this argument is the idea that literary discourse focuses on the creation of language over and above those that are required by the linguistic code. The social situation from which the authors craft their ideas bestows specific roles upon the linguistic, occupational, power relations and importantly identity construction goals.

The interconnectedness between literary discourse and language is intriguing. In an earlier account of the literariness of discourse, Aboh (2013b) notes that, in dealing with literary texts as a form of social discourse, the discourse analyst should be interested in how language describes the events in society and how individual writers' linguistic configurations are a reflection of such events. In a similar vein, Bahri had earlier averred that conceptualising literature as social discourse 'does not imply literature's insularity' (2003, 6); rather, it considers literary text 'within its wider social, cultural, political and historical contexts' (Aboh 2013a, 17). There is the need to see literature as a symbolic stage where the political, social and cultural lives of people interweave with language. A literary text is a stage where writers use language to project their identities and the voices of others; these voices maybe explicit and identifiable or not but they have a mental representation in the discursive architecture of the literary characters. Literary discourse, at least from the perspective followed by this book and from insights drawn from scholars who have taken this line of argument, focuses on how language and society interact, and how this interaction shapes human existence. Fowler (1996, 130) precisely sums up the foregoing argument as he notes that literature 'gives an interpretation of the world it represents'.

It has been ascertained that literature is 'a network of discourse, certain configuration of legitimate speech activities' (Maingueneau 2010, 150).Working against the backdrop of linguists' claim that 'linguistic structure is not arbitrary, but is determined by, or motivated by the functions it performs' (Fowler 198, 28), the analyst of the language of texts must rely on the social and personal needs language is detailed to perform. Therefore, to see literature as discourse is to understand the social situations that backgrounds the production processes of the texts in question. Having drawn attention to the theoretical structures that will guide this study, the author summarises the selected texts in the section that follows.

The selected texts

Chimamanda Ngozi Adichie's *Half of a Yellow Sun* (hereafter *Yellow Sun*), mainly set in southeastern Nigeria, is a fictionalised historical account of Biafra: an examination of the genesis and the eventual collapse of the Biafran nation. We encounter Odenigbo, a revolutionary mathematics lecturer in the University of Nigeria, Nsukka. Odenigbo is very popular within the University community because of his Pan-African identity, total interest in Africa's liberation from colonial and neo-colonial influences and a fascinating humanism. Because of these ideals, he is able to gather a followership of intellectuals. His house becomes a rendezvous for debates on varied international and local issues.

There is also Ugwu, the hero of the novel, who learns fast, loves and serves Master diligently. His diligence and admiration are further deepened as Odenigbo's girlfriend, Olanna, takes up a teaching job with the Department of Sociology and decides to stay in Odenigbo's flat rather than occupy the one allocated to her by the University authorities. Ugwu likes and respects Olanna; and so he does everything to keep the relationship between Olanna and Master intact. He is always there for them; at the time of crises, he comes in and tactically mends some broken walls. Ugwu's admiration for Olanna deepens even much more as he discovers that she speaks Igbo (a sense of ethnic pride). Through his central narrative role, we are made to understand that Olanna's Igbo is softer and featherier than Odenigbo's.

Life in the University goes on interestingly. Ugwu, the village boy, metamorphoses expeditiously into a university boy. Through his quick transformation he graphically tells us everything that happens in Odenigbo's house. He tells us about the gathering of intellectuals in Odenigbo's flat; how each intellectual speaks, drinks, and argues. He dislikes Miss Adebayo because of the disrespectful manner she talks to Odenigbo — her voice is painfully loud, towering higher over Master's. He tells us about Okeoma, the poet who reads his poems to the gathering. Through Ugwu, we encounter the passionate love-making scenes between Odenigbo and Olanna. But such moments of intellectual gathering, peace and solitude are soon to be over because of the news of the coup which is considered an Igbo coup that is targeted at eliminating Hausa leaders. Months later, there is a counter coup. Military officers of Igbo extraction are killed and Igbo civilians resident in the north are killed in their numbers, and many are left with no option but to return to the east — their homeland. The war breaks out, leading to the eventual disintegration of Nigeria.

It is important to mention that *Yellow Sun* gives an account of the sociopolitical development of the Nigerian nation immediately after her independence. It is a narrative that artistically captures the clamour for the control of newly independent Nigeria by the three large ethnic groups: Igbo, Hausa and Yoruba. A reading of

Yellow Sun from inter-ethnic relations will enhance one's understanding of Nigeria's sociopolitical evolution as well as existence. It talks about the inability of Nigerian leaders to handle ethnic differences.

In terms of language-in-use, the focus of this book, *Yellow Sun*, like the other novels sampled for this project, is a clear-cut example of the burden of the Nigerian writer — the language palaver. The need to write about the cultural reality of her Igbo people and her Nigerian nation has prompted the novelist to loan words, code-switch and transliterate, among other linguistic acts, producing a narrative that is replete with Igbo linguistic expressions. These Igbo expressions do not only depict her Igboness, but also the nativisation or 'Nigerianisation' of the English language by Nigerian prose writers. Such linguistic experimentations do not seem to be out of place as they depict her allegiance to her Igbo ethnic identity. This is because she constantly 'intersperses and dignifies her novel with Igbo expressions worked inimitably into the complex tapestry of her narrative' (Anyokwu 2011, 83). The kernel of such linguistic modality is given due attention in the following chapters of this book.

Liwhu Betiang's *The Cradle on the Scale*, (henceforth *The Cradle*) is the story of a bastard boy, Unimke, Betiang's central character. As the story begins, we meet Andoukye, the teenage housemaid with a mysterious pregnancy, and we are made to sympathise with her because of the dehumanisation she suffers in Catechist's house. Andoukye, whose mother died during her birth, is sent by her father, Ukandi, to stay with Catechist. She does not know that Akomaye's, Catechist's first son's, incestuous act is the reason for her early morning sickness. Bottom line: she is pregnant but cannot tell how because she is a teenager who lacks the knowledge of pregnancy; and Akomaye, the one who did it has long returned to school. When he hears the news of Andoukye's pregnancy, Akomaye writes his father, urging him *to do something* about the pregnancy.

After college, Akomaye refuses to go home and remains in Kano, northern Nigeria, because his father failed to solve the mystery of the 'virgin' conception. No one seems to be responsible for Andoukye's pregnancy. There is tension in the family. Catechist's wife, Ungieubua, wants to know how the pregnancy came about. She is restrained from suspecting her husband because she knows that his manliness has 'blackened out'. Ungieubua's characterisation opens up an interesting dimension to gender identity construction in the African context.

The Cradle embodies the cultural practices of the novelist's Bette-Bendi people. It tells us that incest remains a grievous offence. A sacrifice which requires a sheep's blood must be used to cleanse the incestuous family of the evil that will befall it. In the Bette-Bendi cultural practice, the numerous consequences of incest are not suffered by the culprits alone, but the entire community: it can lead to serial misfortune for the community. This is why the cleansing ritual requires the participation of the entire community, pointing to the seamlessness and non-individuation of African communality. That such a belief still finds expression in the novelistic engagement of a twenty-first-century writer suggests that the novelist is saying that his Bette-Bendi beliefs remain sacrosanct despite the unwavering presence of Christianity.

Like many Nigerian novels, Betiang's *The Cradle* is littered with linguistic expressions drawn mainly from his Bette-Bendi language but also from other Nigerian languages, pointing to an ethno-national consciousness. The characterisation process and events in the story provide us with ethnic and cultural information about his Bette-Bendi people and the Nigerian people as a whole. How Betiang uses language to provide information about the Nigerian people is the motivation for the selection of his novel for this work.

Sefi Atta's *A Bit of Difference* (hereafter *Difference*) tells the story of Nigerians both in the diaspora and in Nigeria. It describes the life of urban men and women. It tells the story of Nigerians like Bamidele who, though not doing well, prefer to stay in London. Bamidele's characterisation describes identity loss. He is neither Nigerian nor British. He refuses to return to Nigeria and he is not accepted in London. It is also a tale of people like Dara, a school dropout who ventured into music as an escape route, who are used by some non-governmental organisations (NGOs) to generate funds and are later abandoned once the NGO's objective is achieved. *Difference* captures various shades of racism some Nigerians suffer abroad. Their level of education does not exempt them from being racially debased.

Deola's mother (Atta's strong woman and heroine) is troubled and wants Deola to return to Nigeria where she can find herself a man. On one of her visits to Nigeria, she meets Wale, the owner of the hotel she lodges in. She throws caution to the wind and has sex with him. Back in London, she tests negative for HIV, but positive for pregnancy. Deola is afraid her mother will throw her out. So, she tells Aunty Bisi who helps in calming her mother's nerves because she is already angry with Deola for getting pregnant by a man who has not followed the customary way of marrying a woman. Deola leaves LINK, the organisation she works for in London, and returns to Nigeria to be married. In doing so, she fulfils her community obligation that all must be married and have children.

Difference is about family — the novelist imprints on the mind of her readers that family is cardinal to the sustenance of in-group membership. Deola, for example, is sexually involved with a man she meets for the first time simply because she is pressured by family to get married. The pressure to marry is rooted in the traditional African belief that every woman is expected to be married and have children. So, when a woman who has come of age is yet to be married, she becomes not only the subject of discussion, but of worry to both her immediate family and other members of her community.

Just like *Yellow Sun* and *The Cradle*, Atta's use of language in *Difference* tells us that the book is primarily about the Yoruba people in southwestern Nigeria and the Nigerian people as a whole. It depicts ethnic identity and stereotyping because characters in the novel are encouraged to marry from their ethnic group, reinforcing the reason Deola's mother is not happy that her son, Lanre, is married to Eno, an Efik woman whose people 'eat dogs'. However, Atta's naming practice shows that she favours inter-ethnic cohabitation. Her use of language in *Difference*, just like that of the two other authors, provides cultural information about dress/clothes, religious beliefs and the culinary habits of the Nigerian people. *Difference* thus is ideal for studying in the light of language and identity construction, which serves as motivation for the choice of this book for analysis in the current work.

Having argued that the use of language in the Nigerian novel goes far beyond stylistic motivations, accounted for the connection between language and identity, provided insights into the theoretical considerations for the study, advanced the need for an eclectic analysis of ethnic, cultural, gender and national identities and provided a brief summary of the sampled texts, I move to closely examine, in Chapter 2, how names and naming function as linguistic texts for ethnic identity construction.

2

Constructing ethnic identity

Names as labels of ethnic identity

Identity discourse scholars have written expressive essays emphasising the relationship between language and ethnic identity. The majority of these scholars (e.g. Baker 2001; Ushie and Aboh 2013; De Fina 2007) are of the opinion that an important aspect of ethnic identity is an individual's mother tongue. Although there are factors — cultural and religious — which are identity construction materials, the emotional significance attached to a mother tongue in terms of ethnic identity is usually more heightened than any other identity construction dimension. Pentecostal Christians in Nigeria, for example, identify with people from diverse ethnic groups in Nigeria through the language of Pentecostalism, 'a language commonly associated with new generation Christians' (Aboh 2015b, 512): this can be taken as the symbol of their religious identity. But this Pentecostal language often fails to be a binding force in situations of ethnic clashes. In situations of ethnic crises, as are prevalent in Africa and other continents of the world, religious identity is always set aside, and ethnicity becomes the basis of oneness and otherness. A clearer understanding of ethnicity or ethnic identity construction in Nigerian novels requires a focus on the linguistic as well as a socio-ethnic analysis of how Nigerian novelists deploy linguistic resources to create and negotiate ethnic belonging. The theoretical frame of reference for the study of ethnic identity shows how participants in social activities 'do' identity work and affiliate with or distance themselves from social categories of belonging, depending on the local context of interaction and its insertion in the wider social world (Bucholtz and Hall 2005). In this book, the focus is specifically on the use of names in the construction of ethnic identity.

Names are not the only linguistic means by which ethnic identity is enunciated. However, the striking manner in which they are deployed in the selected texts provides us with eloquent testimonies of how ethnicity and ethnic identities are enunciated using names. The focus in this chapter therefore is on names. There is a deep confluence between names and identity. But, in discussing the use of names as linguistic texts for articulating ethnic identity, other linguistic items that collaborate to depict ethnic differences are equally accounted for. This draws from Joseph's (2004) idea that '[t]he importance of language ... is by no means restricted to the names that get attached to people to indicate their ethnic belonging, but can extend to the way they speak generally' (170). In most African communities, the proper or personal name which a person bears sums up not only their individuality, but significantly their ethnic affiliation. Names are more than labels of identification; they provide us with historical and spiritual/religious, and significantly, ethnic accounts. Names and naming are labels of ethnic identity. Similarly, literary characters' names are mostly drawn from the ethnic culture of the writer. Since they are drawn from the ethnic culture of the writer, names provide readers with the essential ideas of the writer's people and belief systems. Suleiman (2006) too has projected the idea that names are semiotic practices that shed light on issues of ethnic and national identities.

In Chapter 1, it was mentioned tangentially that names have semantic undercurrents, i.e. they 'have clear descriptive meanings' (Isingoma 2014, 87). Isingoma goes on to state that African personal names contain three main elements that can be regarded as lexical semantic classes. The first class of personal names signifies the general circumstances under which a child was born; the second class of personal names expresses the parents'/people's communication of their feelings; and the third class of personal names describes the child's appearance. The names and naming techniques found in the sampled Nigerian novels fit Isingoma's classification schema. However, an aspect Isingoma's classification does not highlight is the angle of ethnic and national identities as pointed out by Suleiman (2004). The fact is that in literary situations writers' use of language can become a conduit through which their ethnic and nationalistic feelings, ideologies and identity are articulated. Put differently, what writers do with the resources of linguistic elements available to them can hardly be differentiated from their perception of the world. Names in literary contexts play this role of linguistic enactment of ideological leaning and the construction of ethnic as well as national identities.

It has been argued that naming is a traditional practice in Africa since it is done in line with the customs of the parents of the child who is being named. Ibukun and Omotosho (2014) are of the opinion that naming is not only an identity marker, but an important signification system in African cosmology. Every name has a semantic as well as a pragmatic value attached to it. This is duly connected with the idea that the naming event or ceremony in most African cultures is executed in line with certain cultural expectations.

Table 2.1 presents the distribution — in frequency and percentage — of names used in the selected texts according to their ethnic ancestry.

Table 2.1 Distribution of names used in the selected texts

Languages	*Yellow Sun*	*Difference*	*The Cradle*	Frequency	%
Igbo	60	3		64	38.0
Hausa	4	4	1	9	5.3
Yoruba	1	30	1	32	19.0
Bette-Bendi	0	0	19	19	11.3
Efik	2	2	1	5	2.9
English	12	14	7	33	19.6
Others	3	3	0	6	3.5

Table 2.1 accounts for the frequency and percentage distribution of names in the sampled texts. This quantitative account is quite significant because it enriches our understanding of how naming systems index identity. When authors assign names to their characters, the primary motivation is not to vary their stylistic choices, but to make the characters represent certain ideological messages. This position will explain itself as the analysis of naming strategies is undertaken.

The languages — Igbo, Yoruba and Bette-Bendi — are the indigenous languages spoken by the three novelists. Generally, Table 2.1 shows that Nigerian novelists use or create characters and assign to them names that are drawn from English, indigenous languages and various other languages. In so doing, the novelists attest to the sociolinguistic truism that Nigeria is a multilingual as well as a multi-ethnic state whose peoples have co-habited for a long time. However, the most interesting aspect of this naming technique is that the novelists each populate their work with characters drawn primarily from their own ethnic language. This is an act of ethnic identity enactment. This is why Igbo, for example, has 38.0% with the names occurring over 60 times in Adichie's *Yellow Sun*. It reveals the novelist's instantiation of her pan-Igbo identity. This linguistic act is not different from what is obtained in her first novel, *Purple Hibiscus*. Yoruba has 19.0%; the majority of the Yoruba names are drawn from Atta's *Difference*, and the reason for this is obvious: the novel is partly set in Lagos. That is however not an excuse for the dominance of names with Yoruba etymology over others. If part of the novel is set in London, and Nigeria is an ex-British colony that uses English as its official language, why do we have more Yoruba names than English ones? Discourse analysts who interrogate the sociological intersection of language and society attempt to answer this kind of question. Having noted this earlier, it is important for the discourse analyst to look beyond aesthetic values for the answer to such a question. The fact is that the dependence on stylistic tools in interrogating such linguistic instantiation of ideas will conduce to nothing but a misunderstanding, if not an undermining, of the social forces that act on writers' linguistic calibration and conceptualisation of ideas. While naming practice is an integral core of a people, it also opens a window to text as performance. The conception of text as performance needs to be supplemented with a multidimensional approach to the study of the confluence between language and identity construction in the Nigerian novel. Thus, multidimensionality will enable the analyst to account for the 'unsaid said' in texts, for there is a subtext to every text.

Another symbolic dimension captured in Table 2.1 is the scarce use of Bette-Bendi names. In fact, all the Bette-Bendi names are only used in Betiang's *The Cradle*. Bette-Bendi, Betiang's indigenous language, is spoken in northern Cross River State, Nigeria. It has one of the smallest numbers of speakers of indigenous languages in Nigeria, even in Cross River State. This is a pointer to the categorisation of Nigerian languages as well as people into the majority and minority paradigm. However, Betiang's use of Bette-Bendi names and their cultural significations, like his counterparts, is an 'act of identity'. He projects the idea that his Bette-Bendi language and origin must be given expression in the wider matrix of his literary output, thereby giving the Bette-Bendi ethnic group a place in Nigeria's complex linguistic map.

A gloss over the use of English names will fail to unveil the primal motive of the dominance of indigenous names over English ones. One expects to have, if not equal, more names from English. Given the multiplicity of indigenous languages in Nigeria, English has remained Nigeria's official language. Moreover, Nigerian writers primarily compose their novels in English. As much as one will not undermine the fact that these novels are about a people and their realities, it is yet interesting to note that two of the sampled authors Adichie and Atta are based in the diaspora. In corollary, one expects that they use more of English names in their creative works than they have done. On the whole, one would say that Table 2.1 does not only illustrate the frequency of the names used in the novels, but points axiomatically to the authors' preference for indigenous names over English ones.

Having undertaken a quantitative analysis of names and naming strategies, it is important to investigate further, from textual examples, the conjunction between naming practices and (ethnic) identity construction. In doing so, the names found in the sampled texts are categorised into three: names that describe the circumstances that surround the birth or coming of a child; those that are ego boosting; and names that perform metadiscursive functions of labelling the 'Other'.

Circumstantial names and naming

The name a child is given interweaves with the conditions that surround the birth of a child. An understanding of the rationale behind why a person was given a particular name is invariably an appreciation of the essential existence of a group of people. Table 2.2 presents some circumstantial names across the selected novels under the beam of this study.

Table 2.2 Circumstantial names

S/N	Name	Gloss	Gender	Origin	Novel
1	Andoukye	Wiper of tears/consoler	F	Bette-Bendi	*The Cradle* (21)
2	Unimke	It is God who gives	M	Bette-Bendi	*The Cradle* (26)
3	Babajide	In honour of a late father	M	Yoruba	*Difference* (217)
4	Adewale	The crown has returned home	M	Yoruba	*Difference* (184)
5	Obianuju	The one who comes in the time off plenty/wealth	F	Igbo	*Yellow Sun* (136)
6	Obiageli	One who comes to enjoy/ spend or eat	F	Igbo	*Yellow Sun* (310)
7	Akomaye	Let me be quiet for the time being	M	Bette-Bendi	*The Cradle* (7)

The names presented in Table 2.2 are primarily drawn from the novelists' indigenous languages. The naming practice displays the novelists' intention to attach value to their respective languages. It does not appear to be out of place to argue that the names carry specific information about the novelists' people's cosmology and their disposition to reality. The Bette-Bendi name, Andoukye, for example, which translates as wiper of tears or one who gives consolation, describes the circumstance that surrounds the birth of the named one. In *The Cradle*, Ukandi, the name giver, tells us why he names his daughter Andoukye:

> She never had a mother; she had died at childbirth — her birth. That's how she came to be called Andoukye: the one who came to console. (Betiang 2011, 21)

Ando means 's/he drove' and *ukye* translates as 'tears'. The shortened form is *Akye*. It is a name that is given specifically to a female child whose parents have experienced hard times, especially the death of a loved one. This is the case in the context of the novel. Ukandi names the child Andoukye because her coming coincides with the death of his wife. In other words, she is a consoler who came to console her father after his wife's, her mother's, death. Another instance in which Andoukye is given to a female child is when the mother has long awaited a child. Most often, as illustrated in the novel, women in the Bette-Bendi region of Nigeria are despised and blamed for not having children (This is discussed in detail in Chapter 5.) So, when a woman finally gives birth to a female child, the husband can give her the name he prefers, but most women call such 'circumstantial' children Andoukye: one who has come to dry up the tears of childlessness. Though it is not the focus of this chapter, it is pertinent to mention here that women are often blamed for 'their inability' to have children and men are exempted without believing that they could have fertility problems. This gender bias is articulated in the way women name their female children.

Another example of how the Bette-Bendi people encode the circumstance that surrounds a named one's birth can be seen in the name Unimke. Andoukye, Unimke's mother, is pregnant. Yet, no one knows who is responsible for her pregnancy. The unborn child has already been seen as a bastard. Unimke, it is God who gives, personifies the Bette-Bendi religious philosophy of the Almighty who has a supreme and final say over people's existence. Ukandi, Unimke's grandfather, clarifies why his grandson is so named:

> She will continue to live in her son, the son Nature has given me. Unimke shall be his name because it is the Almighty that continues to give even as He that takes away from me. (Betiang 2011, 26)

Unim means 'God' while *ke* translates as 'give': therefore, Unimke roughly translates as God's gift. The name incarnates the idea that the Bette-Bendi people believe that all their earthly possessions come from God. Unimke's mother died at childbirth, and he is considered a gift from God. Even when his father is unknown, he is accepted since children naturally come from God. This is why even when Unimke's father, Akomaye, knows that Unimke has been involved in armed robbery and later raped his aunty, Mary, he accepts him since he is a gift from God. Moreover, the novelistic example exposes the hidden belief that when a woman dies during childbirth, her spirit does not part with her but lives in the child. There is an extant conceptualisation of life as a coherent and seamless continuum. This is why Ukandi says *she will continue to live in her son*. This way, the bond between mother and son remains unbroken. This naming practice tells us that the Bette-Bendi people think of life as elastic and interminable; it is continuous and exists in four levels of the living, the dead, the unborn and transition. In fact, commenting on the religious philosophy of Bette-Bendi names, Ushie and Imbua firmly posit that names are important to the Bette-Bendi community because 'names represent the thoughts of a man at a time, his joy, his sorrows, his life situations, his history, his sense of religion, his philosophies, etc' (2011, 253). All these are highlighted in the naming of Unimke.

The reflexivity between the name given and the incident that circumstantiates the birth of a child is also explored in Atta's *Difference*:

> She says if they have a son, she will call him Babajide, to honour his father and hers. He agrees that Jide is a solid traditional name. (Atta 2013, 217)

In the above fragment, Deola, Atta's heroine, is expecting a baby, and she tells Wale that if they have a male child, they will call him Babajide. Before one explains why this is a conscious act of ethnic identity construction, it is worthy to note that Babajide is a name, which, in the Yoruba naming narrative, is given to a male child whose birth comes after the passing on of the child's grandfather or any elderly male member of the extended family. Jide is the shortened form of Babajide. In the context of the novel, both Deola and Wale's parents (but for Deola's mother) have passed on. When Deola suggests the name, Wale agrees that *Jide is a solid traditional name*. Since Yoruba has a strong cultural practice of reverence for elders, the name echoes the Yoruba moral ideology of respect for the elderly. Moreover, it may be argued that the Yoruba people are more greatly attached to their cultural values than any other ethnic group in Nigeria: they hardly take English names, even the most religious ones. Therefore, the motivation for the inclusion of the expression — *Jide is a solid traditional name* — is an enactment of the author's Yoruba ethnic identity. It is also a linguistic instantiation of a way of life the Yoruba people hold dear to themselves. Besides the need for continuity, the underlying import for using the name in Atta's *Difference* is the practice of familial identity retention. The Yoruba people, like the Bette-Bendi people discussed above, believe in the cyclic nature of life: that the living is, in several inexplicable ways, connected with the dead. This philosophical positioning is the theme of Wole Soyinka's (1975) *Death and the King's Horseman*.

In another example, Atta explores the cultural semantic value of Yoruba names and the interconnectedness that exists between names and the situation that informs a child's birth. In the excerpt below, Adewale tells Deola:

> 'No, my mother was not married to my father when I came along. His family didn't actually know I existed until he died. He left me this place. His family wasn't happy about that.'
> 'The Adeniran family?'
> 'Yes. My father is … was J. T. Adeniran. He was a lawyer. I'm his only son.
> (Atta 2013, 184)

Adewale, the crown has returned home, is a name given to male children who naturally inherit or take the place of a father after his passing on. We see how the meaning of the name played itself out in the above example. Although Adewale was not known by other members of the Adeniran family because he is a product of an extramarital affair, he comes back, just as his name says, after his father's death to inherit that which belongs to him. Though it is not the focus of this chapter, attention needs to be drawn to the subtle patriarchal practice of inheritance where women are systematically sidelined from inheriting their father's property. That notwithstanding, the name is rooted in the Yoruba ideology of familial continuity: it is a male child who has the capacity to uphold as well as continue the family's lineage since the woman is often 'married out' and becomes a member of her husband's family. So, Adewale's characterisation fits perfectly well in the naming narrative; as a male child, despite his birth, he returns and takes charge of his father's position as the head of the family.

The circumstantial act of naming is also acutely articulated in Adichie's *Yellow Sun*. Even the revolutionary university intellectual, Odenigbo, appreciates the reflexivity between a named one and a father's situation. He tells Olanna that they should have a little girl and when they have her, she will be called 'Obianuju because she will complete us' (2007, 136). Embedded in Odenigbo's ideology of having a little girl is the notion that for any union between a man and woman to be complete, at least in Nigeria, is to have children. Literally, Obianuju means the one who comes in the time of plenty. But this translation is not invariable as there are many Igbo dialects, and more so, Obianuju is a shortened form of a longer name. It could be Obianujunwa — the one who comes in the fullness of children, i.e. the one who came to meet other children; Obianuju/Obianajuaku — the one who comes to a family at its height of beauty. From the contextual clue, the last of the two glosses of Obianaju fits into the case between Odenigbo and Olanna. Both Odenigbo and Olanna are wealthy and beautiful people, and all they long for is a child. Their desperation for a baby intercepts with the significance the Igbo people, like other groups in Nigeria, place on children. Hence, a union is seen as incomplete without a child no matter how wealthy or successful the people are.

Another subtext to the above example is the sex of the baby. Although there is preference for male children, many fathers can hardly disguise their love for female children. For example, in a conversation between Benyin and Unimke in the novel, *Above the Rubble*, Benyin tells Unimke:

> 'You know what,' she turned and faced Unimke. 'Everyman wants a male child but he is the first to fall head long in love with a female child immediately she is born. The name he gives her is quite often an explication of such love. (Aboh 2015c, 84)

This is a subtle and tacit explanation of what a name means to many a Nigerian man. Adichie, like her counterparts in this study, always makes linguistic comments with Igbo names. She describes events, concepts and ideas that surround the birth of a child with Igbo names and identities. Olanna, for example, rejects Obiageli, the name Odenigbo's mother gave Baby at birth. Olanna rejects the name because she understands the connotation that underlies the naming act. Obiageli, one who comes to enjoy/spend or eat, implies that Baby came to 'eat' her father's wealth. The full form of Obiageli is Obiageliaku. *Aku* means wealth. Mama names the child Obiageli only to spite Olanna who is yet to have her own child. Earlier in the story, Mama had accused Olanna of being a witch who has come to *eat* her son's wealth without giving her son a child, a male one to be specific. Given the background knowledge of the mutual suspicion that exists between Mama and Olanna, Olanna knows that the name is not for the child but targeted at her. In fact, Obiageli is a feminine name but in some cases when a man is derogatively called Obiageli, it means he is lazy and lives off other people.

When Odenigbo tells Olanna that Mama named Amala's daughter Obiageli, Olanna is angry, and she responds:

> 'We can't call her that name.' His mother had no right to name a child she had rejected. 'We'll call her Baby for now until we find the perfect name,'. Kainene suggested Chiamaka. 'I've always loved that name: God is beautiful. Kainene will be her godmother. I have to go see Father Damian about her baptism.' She would go shopping at Kingsway. She would order a new wig from London. She felt giddy. (Adichie 2007, 310)

Considered on a superficial level, the re-naming of Baby will hardly be appreciated. The re-naming does not only reflect the link between name and self, but also how names are deployed culturally to structure our society and how people interpret their 'worlds'. Our conception of names is in every sense connected with our cultural knowledge of our 'worlds'. Mama wants a male child but a female one came. Symbolically, by naming Baby Chiamaka, Olanna constructs the idea that it is God who gives children: male and female. Critically examined, the name echoes Olanna's perception of children. She also passes the message that she will have a child when God, who is beautiful, wants her to have one. Moreover, to call a child Baby, a name that can be used to identify either of the sexes means that the child does not have an identity. It also addresses the circumstance that brought Baby to existence. She is a product of the ill-informed liaison between Odenigbo and Amala. The name connotes rejection. When she is delivered, Baby is rejected by Mama. Importantly, Baby's high-pitched cry as Olanna takes her from Odenigbo is metadiscursively symbolic and deeply psychological. It explains Baby's awareness of her rejection by her own mother and her grandmother. Psychologically, though the child cannot talk, it amplifies the child's bitterness that circumstantiated her birth.

This philosophical conjecture is also seen in the name Akomaye. Akomaye, a name given to a male child whose parents have long awaited a child, translates as 'I withhold my joy/let me suppress for the time being my joy', describes a father's astonishment at the good things that have happened to or around him. This often describes those who have been written off. In other words, the father, by naming a son Akomaye, is asking, 'Is it true that I am a father, not a mere man?' This is seen in the Betiang's *The Cradle* as Akomaye's father did not believe he was going have a child because of the problem he and his wife had had concerning childbirth. An implicit meaning to the name Akomaye is its clinical explication of a masculinist African worldview where childlessness is often blamed on a woman. In most instances, in-laws, especially mothers-in-law, are always at war with daughters-in-law for failing to give them a son. A woman can give her son who came after such a 'war of childlessness' the name. In such a circumstance, the name carries the illocutionary force of consoling a mother as well as warning her provocateurs who had chided her for not having children.

It can be surmised that besides explaining the novelists' ethnic identity, the names and naming practices discussed above describe factual circumstances surrounding name giving, givers and the named one. Perhaps it is not audacious to conclude that personal names in Bette-Bendi, Yoruba, Igbo, as have other ethnic groups in Nigeria, are significant identity markers; for these names tell the story of the name giver. For example, Obiannujuaka, the one who came to a family at the fullness of wealth/riches, tells the story that the child's parents are accomplished, are wealthy and all they desire is a child that will complete them, just as Odenigbo tells Olanna. The implication is that the study of names or naming practices as a linguistic activity is invariably a study of the ethnic undercurrents of a people's philosophical disposition to existence.

Personality promotion/Ego-boosting names

> I know Nabal is a wicked and ill-tempered man; please don't pay any attention
> to him. He is a fool as his name suggests. (1 Samuel 25:25, NLT)

In the preceding section, the focus was on how names and naming practices are calibrated in line with the circumstances that bespeak a child's birth. In this way, the symbolic conjunction between the events that preceded a child's birth and the name given to the child by the name giver is a common naming practice in most African communities. Therefore, when one hears a particular name and if that person speaks and understands the language of the named one, the person can tell what the parents of the child went through or the prevalent situation in the parents' community before or during the period the child came along.

Another category or class of names worthy of explanation in this chapter is personality or ego-boosting names. These are names assigned to a child to identify it with the traits it portrays as well as the personality (social identity) of the child's parents. In other words, some names are intended to boost a parent's ego and also speak into the child's life, directing it on the path of life to follow. This suggests that naming, as a culturally determined activity that thrives on the resources of language, is not done haphazardly: every name is a label, an emblem that defines people's behaviour. This is largely psychological. Table 2.3 represents names and naming systems that are meant to boost or promote either the parents' ego or steer the child's life in a particular direction.

Table 2.3 Ego-boosting names

S/N	Name	Gloss	Gender	Origin	Novel
1	Odenigbo	Son of the soil	M	Igbo	*Yellow Sun* (25)
2	Ugwuanyi	The mountain/hill is not impossible/insurmountable	M	Igbo	*Yellow Sun* (216)
3	Ukongben	She who speaks her mind	F	Bette-Bendi	*The Cradle* (80)
4	Olanna	Father's jewel	F	Igbo	*Yellow Sun* (78)
5	Adeola	A crown of wealth	F	Yoruba	*Difference* (52)
6	Jaiye	The child should enjoy life	F	Yoruba	*Difference* (69)
7	Ogbenyealu	To be married to a wealthy man	F	Igbo	*Yellow Sun* (91)
8	Lanre	Wealth is progressing	M	Yoruba	*Difference* (73)
9	Ungieubua	The light/fair-skinned woman	F	Bette-Bendi	*The Cradle* (45)

A person's name can play itself out in the individual's outlook or in the way the person responds to the issues of life. The meaning of the name, Odenigbo, son of the soil, manifests itself in the life of the university lecturer. Throughout the novel, Odenigbo boasts of being the 'son of the soil'. It is part of this cultural nationalism that makes him insist:

> 'Odenigbo. Call me Odenigbo'.
> Ugwu stared at him doubtfully. 'Sah?'
> 'My name is not *Sah*. Call me Odenigbo'.
> 'Yes, sah'.
> 'Odenigbo will always be my name. Sir is arbitrary. You could be *sir* tomorrow.'
> (Adichie 2007,25)

In *Yellow Sun*, we encounter Odenigbo who is passionately and tendentiously involved in the Biafran cause. He is in full support of Biafra secession because he thinks that northern Nigeria has treated his Igbo people badly. Odenigbo constructs this pan-Igbo ethnic identity throughout the novel. For instance, he consistently reminds Ugwu to *call me Odenigbo* (2007,29). Boasting names have a way of refocusing one's perspective. This is the reason Odenigbo, despite the fact that he studied abroad, prefers to speak Igbo except when he is with those who do not speak the language. There is an imprint of his name in the entire characterisation process. Odenigbo is a core traditionalist. His inability to give his mother a befitting burial breaks him and changes his life. He is so obsessed with grief that he could also die trying to bury his mother. Okeoma tells Olanna, *Odenigbo has never known how to be weak. Be patient with him* (2007,392). Though gallant, his mother's death shatters Odenigbo.

Names then, core names to be specific, are not just some arbitrary exercise, but a conscious linguistic activity which helps people to relate with the characteristic trait of the named one. The Yoruba name, Jaiye, the shortened form of Jaiyeola, the child should enjoy life, is a name given to a female child whose parents must have been through some difficult times, poverty, for example; but who later became rich or wealthy. Jaiye, as a name, entails that all the child needs to do is to live and enjoy the father's wealth. Deola, Jaiye's elder sister, tells us in *Difference* that:

> Jaiye was Daddy's girl. He called her 'Doc'. He was worried that her marriage to Funsho would not last. He gave them the house in Ikeja as a wedding present anyway, but he made sure the house was in Jaiye's name alone. (Atta 2013, 69)

It can be inferred from the above extract that even when Jaiye is 'married out', her father ensures that she enjoys his wealth while in her husband's house. But, most importantly, the name describes the fact that Jaiye's father is rich, the owner of Trust Bank. All through the novel, we see Jaiye doing nothing but depicting the fact that she comes from a wealthy home. Even when she was a child, she was taken care of by Deola, and *she grew up and began to preen and read magazines like Vogue and Harpers and Queen* (Atta 2013,68). The most important factor to be considered is the underlying message the name carries: demonstrate my father's wealth. This kind of naming practice in which a child is praised is known as *oriki* in Yoruba. It does not only reflect hopes for the child, but also affirms the child's personality in the community.

Giving an individual a name puts a social emblem on the person. As much as a name identifies a person or speaks for the person, it is symbolic of personal identity. It categorically tells who the named person is and more importantly, it tells the named one what it is expected to do in life. This psycho-cultural paradigm is expressed in the life of Ugwu. Ugwu is one of Adichie's central figures. Through the name bestowed on him, Ugwu is symbolically brought forth as a hero, who is conscripted into the Biafran army. His gallantry becomes even much more epic as he rejects the war and finds his way back to Odenigbo and Olanna. This feat is not achieved by others, Kainene, for example, whose whereabouts remains unknown at the end of the novel.

Before Ugwu's heroic identity display is explained, it is relevant to provide the meaning of his Igbo name. Ugwu may be the shortened form of Ugwuanyionyeso (a runner). The list is endless. But for the purpose of this book, the second meaning — Ugwanyidike (a warrior) is preferred since Ugwu's behaviour throughout the narrative resonates with the ideals of a warrior. His given name continues to highlight itself throughout his evolution. He goes through a multifaceted transformational process: from a village boy through a houseboy to becoming a teacher in the school Olanna sets up during the war and fighting the war in every ramification. His name illustrates milestones along a pathway of change. It must be stated that the bravery demonstrated by Ugwu is an act of ethnic identity construction. The novelist deliberately structures Ugwu the way she does in order to tell her readers that Igbo people are warriors. Adichie narrates how:

> Ugwu knew the story from Pastor Ambrose was implausible, that some people from a foundation abroad had set up a table at the end of St. John's Road and were giving away boiled eggs and bottles of refrigerated water to anyone who passed by. He knew, too, that he should not leave the compound; Olanna's warnings echoed in his head. But he was bored. It was sticky hot and he hated the ashy taste of the water stored in a clay pot behind the house …And the story could well be true; anything was possible. (Adichie 2007,424)

Ugwu is aware of the imminent danger of leaving the compound — it was a time boys were conscripted into the military. Yet, he leaves the compound. He explicitly demonstrates gallantry by leaving the compound. As his name signifies, nothing is insurmountable and *anything is possible*, he assures himself as would a warrior. Therefore, the transformational process undergone by Ugwu is etched in the Igbo ideology of bravery. Bravery is rooted in the canonical supposition that for one to be called a 'man', one has to be courageous and take risks. This explains the factuality that naming is not only an important component of identity, but also provides information about where the name has its roots in. Ugwu is one of Adichie's finest creations: for example, through his characterisation he makes us understand that rape is a violent psychological crime. So, he would do anything to avoid rape of any form.

So far, the stream of argument that has been maintained in this chapter is that there is a dialectical relationship between a person's name and the person's behaviour. In fact, Le Page and Tabouret-Keller (1985) insightfully describe how an act of identity is to reveal an individual's identity and to search for a social role. The Bette-Bendi name Angwubua, the fair-skinned one or a white person, for example, tells us what he does:

> She hesitated at the door and called out. 'Are you in?' A voice answered in affirmation from within and she entered.
> 'Lady, my lady, how was the market today?'
> 'No money in the country, nobody buys, nobody sells.'
> 'Na so my Sister, when they don thieve the money spoil country, them blame economy.' He chorused as he sat her down beside him in the usual manner. He was big and square-chested, a fellow tailor and chairman of the Tailors Association in the local market. Also a lay-pastor, he was as fair as an

albino; hence popularly known as *Angwubua* meaning the White one.

'I want to go home.' She reminded him.

'I did not ask you to sleep overnight in my shop, did I?' His coarse hands began to fondle her and she giggled like an innocent schoolgirl.

'Oh! Don't do that,' she moaned even as her eyes closed in unconscious desire. (Betiang 2011, 44–45)

Angwubua and Ungieubua, Catechist's wife, are involved in extramarital sex. This can come under the category of nicknames, for nicknames are also ego-boosting names. But an interesting aspect of nicknames functioning as ego-boosting or character depicting names is how people's perception of others is obviated through the nicknames they give them. In the Bette-Bendi naming system, from which Angwubua is taken, the name is used derogatorily to identify him with the clandestine sexual affair he engages in with someone else's wife, constituting a blot on his escutcheon. Angwubua is not a core Bette-Bendi name, but a name his community assigns him because of his looks.

The inference that can be drawn from the above is that people's behaviour is understood and interpreted in terms of the labels we give them. Windt-Val agrees with the foregoing summation as he argues that '[t]he main condition for the reader to empathise [or dismiss] fully with a literary work is that he or she is able to identify with the character of the novel' (2012, 277–278). This explication of the aggregation of real life people and fictionalised people is captured in the name Ogbenyealu. In Chapter 1, I briefly explained how the name Ogbenyealu echoes the economic ideology of the Igbo people. But it was mentioned that Ogbenyealu is also a self-image building name. To call one's daughter Ogbenyealu is to praise her qualities as a girl. More importantly, it means a woman who will never to be married to a poor man. It also suggests that bride price will bring plenty wealth to her parents. But the underlying ideology of the name, just as in the name, Jaiye, discussed earlier, is to boast that the named one's parents are rich, and anyone who wants to identify with the family, as in marrying their daughter, must equally be rich. The naming strategy reveals the power behind naming rather than just the power in naming. Since an individual's personality can be gleaned from the person's name, it follows that the discourse analyst must take a critical analytical path, an approach that enables the analyst to watch out for the meaning behind the name, not just the meaning in the name. Having explored names that are concerned with boosting the ego/personality of a person, names with ethnic and racial meanings are discussed next.

Names with anti-ethnic/racial sentiments

From the outset of this chapter, it was mentioned that the way names are used in the Nigerian novel instantiates ethnic identity. One thing that has not been critically examined, but mentioned in passing, is the sparse use of English names and those which are not from the novelists' respective indigenous languages. Even when there is scanty use of English names and names from other ethnic groups, they are used with sinister intentions. These names basically express anti-ethnic/racial sentiments. Anti-ethnic/racial sentiments, as used in this book, describe an enactive dissonance or dislike by members of one ethnic/racial group for members of other ethnic/racial groups. Expressions of dislike come in handy in multi-ethnic/racial settings and such expressions are usually contemptuous.

Names, even on the personal level, can function as an arena where opposing ethnic/racial identities manifest. The choice of a name and the role assigned to a character, including the description of the named person, should not be overlooked, especially in a multi-ethnic Nigerian society where ethnic loyalty overshadows national consciousness, on the one hand, and the ways Nigerians have responded to naming in the postcolonial era, on the other. The ways we describe other people and the things we make them do in our characterisation processes, can hardly be differentiated from the opinion we have about them and where they come from. The opinion can be positive or negative or both simultaneously. If we have negative opinions about people, we do not only end up in presenting them as bad people, we also succeed in traducing or devaluing them. In line with the foregoing, Hagstrom's argues that '[t]o have your own name questioned is to be questioned as a person' (2012, 82). In the sampled texts, informed by ethnic and racial sentiments, characters have their identity questioned through the names they are assigned. As Table 2.4 illustrates, those with questionable and demeaning identity are those who are not from the novelists' ethnic/racial groups. To appreciate the anti-ethnic sentiments of some of the names found in the sampled texts, their origin, ordinary meaning and the associated meaning they acquire in the context-of-use are presented in Table 2.4. The contextualised meanings are significant because they reveal the sinister anti-ethnic/racial connotations with which they are imbued.

Table 2.4 Names depicting anti-ethnic/racial sentiments

S/N	Name	Origin	Gloss	Contextual meaning	Novel
1	Adebayo	Yoruba	The crown meets joy	Disrespectful, talkative lady	*Yellow Sun* (32)
2	Okon	Efik/Ibibio	Born at night	House help	*Yellow Sun* (89)
3	Eno	Efik/Ibibio	God's gift	Lazy housewife/ dog eater	*Difference* (105, 106)
4	Harrison	English	Son of Harry	Hater of his culture	*Yellow Sun* (138)

S/N	Name	Origin	Gloss	Contextual meaning	Novel
5	Monday	English	The second day of the week	Smelly, dirty driver	*Difference* (77)
6	Nwachukwu	Igbo	Child of God	A fraudster	*Difference* (95, 130)
7	Nneka	Igbo	Mother is supreme	Pretentious whore	*The Cradle* (30, 32)
8	Esther	Hebrew	Secret/hidden	Adulterous woman	*The Cradle* (172)

The name Adebayo, the crown meets joy, a Yoruba name, is contextualised to mean a disrespectful, loud and talkative woman. Ugwu does not mince words as he tells us about Miss Adebayo and his dislike for her, a dislike that is coated with ethnic prejudice:

> The loudest was Miss Adebayo. She was not an Igbo woman; Ugwu could tell from her name … He did not want to ride in her car, did not like how her voice rose above Master's in the living room, challenging and arguing. He often fought the urge to raise his own voice from behind the kitchen door and tell her to shut up. (Adichie 2007, 32)

By alluding to the fact that Miss Adebayo is 'not an Igbo woman', Adichie gives one the impression that Ugwu's resentment of Miss Adebayo feeds from the notion that she is Yoruba. Also, he hates her because of the way she talks, making one feel that Miss Adebayo does not have a modicum of respect for people, especially his Master, Odenigbo. Ugwu's dislike for Miss Adebayo is heightened such that he only comes short of walking her out of the living room. One is equally left to wonder why she is the only one Ugwu singles out for description. The first thing Ugwu hits at is her name and where she comes from. The obvious basis of Ugwu's resentment of Miss Adebayo is where she comes from — the Yoruba ethnic group. Moreover, if ethnic consciousness is 'described as that subconscious or conscious identification with one's ethnic background' (Obioha 1999 cited in Mbakogu 2002, 199), it implies that Ugwu's description and attitude towards Miss Adebayo is linked to anti-ethnic sentiment. He tells us more about her in a pejorative manner:

> she began to look more and more like a fruit bat, with her pinched face and cloudy complexion and print dresses that billowed around her body like wings. Ugwu served her drinks last and wasted long minutes drying his hands on a dishcloth before he opens the door to let her in. (Adichie 2007, 34)

The above debased description highlights Ugwu's antipathy towards Miss Adebayo. His contempt for her is deep-seated and pathological. He, through carefully selected progressive and comparatives, tells us that her ugliness is progressive — she began to look more and more like a fruit bat. To liken someone to a fruit bat, an ugly mammal, is to dehumanise the person. The animosity is so deeply rooted that he will not ride in her car even when she offers to give him a lift. He prefers walking home to driving in her car; he serves her drinks last and wastes time before he opens the door to let her in. He does not want Odenigbo to be sexually involved with her. One begins to wonder if there is nothing positive or appealing about Miss Adebayo. The fact is that in 'performing' anti-ethnic sentiment, discourse actors employ demeaning and uncouth adjectives in order to present members of the opposing group in negative ways. Hence, the linguistic expressions are usually disaffiliating while describing the perceived antagonistic other.

It is necessary to look closely at Ugwu's description of Olanna vis-à-vis Miss Adebayo:

> Not even the white man Professor Lehman, with his words forced out through his nose sounded as dignified as Master. Master's English was music, but what Ugwu was hearing now, from this woman, was magic. Here was a superior tongue, a luminous language, the kind of English he heard on Master's radio, rolling out with clipped precision. It reminded him of slicing a yam with a newly sharpened knife, the easy perfection in every slice. (Adichie 2007,36)

With the above expressive and captivating account of Olanna, there is the natural propensity for one to like her, if not fall in love with her. Ugwu is fascinated by the way she speaks, far better than Odenigbo whose English is more musical than even the white man, Professor Lehman. It can be seen that Ugwu's description of Olanna is replete with strong, associative and expressive adjectives: *superior tongue, a luminous language, clipped precision* and *easy perfection*, successfully painting the image of a goddess. Juxtaposed with the adjectives he employs to describe Miss Adebayo: *fruit bat, pinched face, cloudy complexion* and *print dresses*, it is glaring that Miss Adebayo is not Olanna's equal and leaves nothing for one to desire. Critically, Olanna's *superior tongue* clarifies that she is superior to Miss Adebayo, a Yoruba lady. The expression, *superior tongue*, is metadiscursive: it is Ugwu's linguistic performance of ethnic dismembering. He passes the message that the Igbo tongue is not only superior to Yoruba, but also to English. In so doing, Ugwu's ethnic display constitutes another layer of identity construction: racial identity. Besides the fact that Olanna's *Igbo words were softer than her English...* (Adichie 2007,36), Ugwu also dismisses Professor Lehman as his words, which are forced out, are not as dignified as those of Master. In this way, Ugwu subtly projects the idea that Igbo is a better language than both English and Yoruba.

If a historiographical account is to be followed, it could be said that Ugwu's behaviour can hardly be disconnected from the ethnic rivalry between the Igbo and the Yoruba specifically and among ethnic groups in Nigeria generally. It is this rivalry that informs Ugwu's disaffection towards Miss Adebayo so that even after the war he wonders, *couldn't Miss Adebayo understand that it was best to go back to Lagos and leave them alone* (Adichie 2007, 509). While it can be said that Ugwu's linguistic choices are dissociative, since he admonishes Miss Adebayo to *leave them alone* to probably face their defeat and return to Lagos where she belongs — a Yoruba region — it also shows how ethnicity and the politicisation of identity predominate at the expense of a pan-Nigerian consciousness. Adichie, as have other novelists, foregrounds such ethnic sentiments not with the intention of promoting them, but to let her readers know that ethnicity is the bane of Nigeria's development.

It can be said that, at least from the analysis undertaken here, that naming is a linguistic means of enacting ethnic identity. In fact, Jowitt asserts that:

> It is possible to say that, in general, Nigerians perceive language as a mark of ethnicity, and that, where their perceptions of the political aspirations of the major ethnic power blocks are concerned, the promotion of the ethnic language connotes the promotion of the corresponding ethnic group itself. (1995, 42)

Jowitt's postulation summarises Nigerian's perception of language. This ethnic difference and awareness that defines inter-ethnic relations in Nigeria's public space is also illuminated in Atta's *Difference*. Deola is sent to Nigeria by her Organisation, LINK, to audit two NGOs: Mrs. Rita Nwachukwu's WIN and Dr. Sokoya's Malaria Organisation. According to Deola's account, Dr. Sokoya is involved in a legitimate and genuine enterprise because:

> Dr. Sokoya introduces her to his employees, a skinny graduate and a woman her age who wears a wig. Deola is pleased that he is not particularly well dressed and doesn't have an expensive car parked outside. The security guards know what he does for a living. This points to the legitimacy, though she is certain he setup the NGO to create a job for himself. (Atta 2013, 73)

While Deola agrees that Dr. Sokoya's NGO is legitimate, she thinks differently of Mrs. Nwachukwu's WIN. Back in London, Deola, trusting and depending on the information Elizabeth, Rita's assistant, gave her, tells Kate:

> 'They are not organised at WIN,' she says. 'Rita wants something and Elizabeth wants something else. Elizabeth was talking to me about a microfinance scheme. She didn't want to involve Rita, but I promised her I would follow up with you.'
>
> Kate sighs. 'I got a phone call from Rita while you were there. She said she would like to meet me when she comes here. She's quite keen. She seems really nice.' (Atta 2013, 131)

It can be deduced from Deola's report that Mrs. Nwachukwu's WIN is illegitimate, a deceitful set up. One is made to wonder if *a skinny graduate* and *he is not particularly well dressed and doesn't have an expensive car parked outside* symbolise sincerity. Kate's response suggests that Deola is biased. It is important to point out that the cordiality, informed by the ethnic attachment, between Deola and Dr. Sokoya, is apparently absent in the conversation between Deola and Rita. The conversational exchange is presented below:

> 'You are Yoruba?'
> 'My mother is Yoruba'
> 'So gbo Yoruba?' [Do you understand Yoruba?]
> 'Mo gbo Yoruba.' [I understand Yoruba.]
> 'I'm surprised.'
> She ignores his putdown, but he grows more inquisitive.
> 'You grow up in Lagos?'
> 'Yes.' (Atta 2013, 72)

It then can be said that Deola's positive report of Dr. Sokoya's malaria NGO has an ethnic undertone: the fact that both of them have Yoruba connections. Because of the embedded ethnic connection, the conversation between Deola and Dr. Sokoya went on smoothly. It can be argued that Deola's smooth interaction with Dr. Sokoya is practically worked out from ethnic sentiment where cultural traits, shared group history and language are factors which inform solidarity and oneness or 'we-ness'. Similarly, the exchange between Deola and Mrs. Nwachukwu leaves one wondering if the two women had a bad history before their encounter.

> 'Are you Yoruba or Hausa?' Mrs. Nwachukwu asks.
> Deola smiles. 'Does it matter?'
> 'Just out of curiosity. "Deola" is Yoruba, but "Bello" could be Hausa.'
> 'It is not Hausa.' (Atta 2013, 90)

It is glaring that there is no love lost between the ethnically estranged women. Deola did not snap at Dr. Sokoya when he asked her whether she was Yoruba, but got irritated when asked the same question by Mrs. Nwachukwu. Besides the fact that there are two ethnic groups that are disaffected with each other, the naming technique is indicative of how names can serve as texts for ethnic identity construction.

This kind of ethnic debasement is also depicted in the deployment of the name, Eno. In *Difference*, Eno, Lanre's wife, despite what she does, is still despised by Mrs. Bello, her mother in-law. On her father in-law's birthday, Eno cooked a pot of *edikangikong* (*edikangikong* is discussed Chapter 3) to honour her father-in law, Mr. Bello, but Mrs. Bello trivialises Eno's effort. She employs demeaning expressions to trivialise Eno's magnanimous show of love:

> … Deola's mother [Mrs. Bello] tried only a teaspoon of the stew and asked,
> 'Don't they eat dogs in Calabar?'

Suddenly, she was suspicious of unidentifiable meats. She who wouldn't hesitate to cook an endangered species of animal. (Atta 2013, 106)

Two items are worthy of critical explanation: one, Mrs. Bello's hypocrisy and sententious comments; two, the pronominal selection, *they*. In the first instance, Mrs. Bello's judgmental attitude and her suspicion of *unidentifiable meats* is connected with Eno's ethnic group. Besides such disparaging stereotyping that is a feature of ethnic identity construction, it is an apt portrayal of how living in Nigeria is marked by ethnic differences. In the second instance, in identity discourse, pronouns are strategically selected to enact antagonism to non-members of a (ethnic) group. The pronoun, *they*, shows antipathy to the Efik, the ethnic group Eno represents. In her utilisation of *they*, Mrs. Bello metadiscursively distances herself from an ethnic group that eat dogs. Therefore, Mrs. Bello's use of language echoes the socio-ethno-linguistic principle that language is a vehicle through which the unique character of a group is expressed and activated to uphold common ethnic ties. Mrs. Bello's abhorrence for Eno is strongly steeped in ethnic sentimentalism. In an earlier encounter with Eno's family, Mrs. Bello laments: *Well, this is what happens when you go and marry someone from somewhere* (Atta 2013, 106). This is a clear testimony of anti-ethnic expression, for to describe where an individual comes from as *somewhere* is not only to devalue the person, but to pass the message that wherever the person comes from is inferior. Yet again, the verb *go* has an underlying signification: to *go* is to leave behind, to abandon. By marrying Eno, Lanre has *abandoned* his Yoruba-ness and taken up an Efik identity — that of an inferior ethnic group.

How the circumstance that surrounds the birth of a child determines the name the child ends up with and the value both the name giver and the named one attach to the given name were emphasised earlier in the chapter. In the context of the selected novels, the way the Efik/Ibibio name is used undermines its cultural and semantic significance. Eno's personal identity is undermined and the ethnic significance the name holds is degenerated. Eno is of mixed parentage: her mother is English and her father, Efik from Cross River State in south-south Nigeria. She is considered a gift to the union of her parents. But Mrs. Bello rather sees Eno as a lazy lady who cannot cook, and Lanre, Eno's husband, laments to Deola, his sister, how Eno does nothing and is *getting fatter and fatter* and *never uses enough pepper* (Atta 2013, 64) when she cooks. Lanre's position describes how primordial values can hinder inter-ethnic relations, culminating in inter-ethnic hostility. Nigerians' identity display then can best be understood from two interconnected perspectives: dual citizenship. They naturally see themselves, first, as belonging to an ethnic group; and second, to a nation — Nigeria. This ambivalent consciousness plays itself out in the manner Nigerian novelists put language to use.

The devaluing of an ethnic identity worked out through naming techniques is not restricted to *Yellow Sun* and *Difference*; it is also enunciated in Betiang's *The Cradle*. Nneka, mother is supreme, is discursively constructed as a whore; and Ugar, having slept with Nneka, tells Akomaye:

> '... Who wants an old weather-beaten over sampled hag? Man ... Who does?'
>
> 'You call Nneka an old over-sampled hag?'
>
> 'Why not? She's cheap, she's worn out from excess sampling and when she feels she realises she's running out of time, she now remembers she's got someone to hook for a life time. Crash-landing; I call that, man!' (Betiang 2011, 33–34)

As can be seen from the foregoing, just as in the example discussed earlier, the undermining of one ethnic group by another is often characterised by disaffiliating vocabulary choices. Ugar describes Nneka with the following identity 'reducing' expressions: *Old weather-beaten over sampled hag and cheap and worn out*. But when it comes to describing Agianye, a girl from his ethnic group, Ugar employs appealing and witty expressions: *a real girl* (Betiang 2011, 32) and *a veritable virgin with all the parts intact* (Betiang 2011, 33). It is therefore easy to want to affiliate with Agianye and disaffiliate with Nneka. Agianye, despite being in an environment that is *ravaged, violated God-forsaken* (Betiang 2011, 33), an environment that encourages promiscuity, is disciplined enough to keep her virginity. Motivated by her 'purity', Ugar does not hesitate to propose to her. In a discursive move, Ugar imprints on our mind the idea that girls who are from his Bette-Bendi ethnic group are reserved and pure whereas Igbo girls, as represented by Nneka, are *worn out* from *over sampling*. It is expedient to note that this kind of ethnic bias resides in many Nigerians' mental architecture and often becomes materials which they rely in the construction of ethnic identity.

Another dimension to naming, as gleaned from the sampled texts, is the strategic deployment of names as text for racial identity construction. In *Difference*, there is the activation of racial discourse through the name, Monday. The character, Monday, has a 'filthy' identity imposed on him by Mrs. Bello. Although she needs his service, Mrs. Bello will not continue to keep Monday because he is unhygienic. She tells Deola:

> 'If only I didn't have to sack my driver.' Her mother says, giving up. 'The fellow had body odour, such awful body odour. I gave him antiseptic soap to wash, but he never made use of them'.
>
> His name was Monday. Her mother also made him disinfect the steering wheel before she drove her car because he didn't always wash his hands after using the toilet. (Atta 2013, 77)

Mrs. Bello had to sack Monday, because for her, he was a dirty fellow who could not be 'managed'. As evident in all the sampled texts, almost all the characters with English names: Peter, Moses and Esther in *The Cradle* (Betiang 2011, 105, 106, 172); George and Comfort in *Difference* (Atta 2013, 10, 129); and Alice, Pastor Ambrose and Charles in *Yellow Sun* (Adichie 2007, 398, 406, 444), are constructed in ways that portray them as having one questionable characteristic or another. In *The Cradle*, for example, Esther is constructed as an adulterous woman:

> This unfortunate day, Akpetel — who delighted in practical jokes, saw Esther's nocturnal visitor enter her house as soon as Pastor left …But to his greatest consternation, he met his wife with a strange nocturnal visitor, right on his holy matrimonial bed… Meanwhile as soon as Esther saw her husband turn their bedroom key, she had started shouting rape! (Betiang 2011,173–174)

We are presented with a woman, Esther, who indulges in extramarital sex. In fact, she has a constant *nocturnal* sexual partner who is unknown to her husband, a pastor. Esther, given her ties with a pastor, is expected to behave in a manner that resonates with religious nobility. The biblical account of the Jewish lady, Esther, tells us of her noble behaviour but the reverse is the case with the Esther in Betiang's *The Cradle*. In terms of racial identity construction, religion is also a distinguishing feature — a feature that differentiates one race from another. Therefore, in socially constructing Esther as an adulterous woman, the novelist succeeds in degrading the Christian religion, on the one hand, and promotes his Traditional African Religion, on the other. The underlying message that women from his ethnic group do not indulge in extramarital sex is rather impressionistic or, if they do, it is not abominable but a way of life. This can be deduced from the mild way the novelist evinces the extramarital sex between Angwubua and Ungieubua. From the handling of Ungieubua's affair with Angwubua, it seems the novelist excuses her inaction. Betiang gives one the impression that it is ideal for Ungieubua to seek external sexual fulfilment since *her husband's power blacked out* (Betiang 2011, 45).

Esther is ethnically constructed, given the identity that is 'alien' to her Bette-Bendi people. Whether Bette-Bendi people involve themselves in extramarital sex or not, the author's creation of Esther derives from feelings and personal beliefs; he creates the belief that it is genetic for 'Esthers' to have sexual affairs outside marriage and such sexual behaviour, as depicted by the novelist, is diametrically opposed to Bette-Bendi culture. Creating Esther's identity reminds one of the sociologists, Omi and Winant's (1994), racial concept of social structure and cultural representation. Also, this kind of construction where non-Nigerians are presented as those who find pleasure in amoral sexual relationships is told by Deola:

> 'Go on,' Graham, growls.
> 'You slob,' Kate says, brushing the sugar out of his beard with her fingers.

> Kate and Graham flirt incessantly… Today, Kate barely taps his arm after she cleans up his beard and he cries out, 'Ow! Did you see that, Delia?'
>
> 'I saw nothing,' Deola says, stepping back into her office.
>
> She overhears Kate saying, 'Graham, don't!'
>
> This is another workplace symbiosis that amuses her, married employees seeking attention from each other, even when they are ill-matched. (Atta 2013, 19–20)

Both Kate and Graham are married people who are sexually involved with each other and they seem to see nothing wrong with it. Deola is rather alarmed because it is unethical. From the foregoing discussion, it can be said that the use of names to express racial difference authenticates the widely followed view that race is both linguistically and socially constructed. Deola steps back into her office and that gives the twosome the opportunity to flirt — 'Graham, don't!' Whatever Kate is trying to stop Graham from doing, the context tells us that he must have touched some sensitive part of her body. Deola chooses to see *nothing* because, so long as she is concerned, it is inappropriate for a man to be sexually involved with another man's wife.

In another example taken from *Yellow Sun*, there is the use of the name, Harrison as a vehicle of racial *othering*. Harrison is Richard's house boy. He is Igbo but prefers European ways to his real Igbo identity. So often, he tries to make his food 'European'. On a particular occasion, Richard takes some food Harrison cooked to the usual gathering at Odenigbo's house. But the food becomes a basis for racial antagonism:

> 'I know those are sausage rolls, but what are these things?' Odenigbo was poking at the tray Richard brought; Harrison had daintily wrapped everything in silver foil.
>
> 'Stuffed garden eggs, yes?' Olanna glanced at Richard.
>
> 'Yes. Harrison has all sorts of ideas. He took out the insides and filled them with cheese, I think, and spices'.
>
> 'You know the Europeans took out the insides of an African woman and then stuffed and exhibited her all over Europe?' Odenigbo asked.
>
> The other guests laughed. Odenigbo did not. 'It's the same principle at play,' he said. 'You stuff food, you stuff people. If you don't like what is inside a particular food, then leave it alone, don't stuff it with something else. A waste of garden eggs, in my opinion'. (Adichie 2007, 138–139)

It is apparent that the above conversation is steeped in racial conflict. Harrison is Richard's houseboy who has 'sorts of ideas' of becoming or being white in all he does. He prefers to speak in English even with his fellow Igbo people — Jomo, the gardener, for example — as a way of socially constructing a 'white' identity for himself. In so doing, he practically relegates his 'Igbo-ness' to the background: a source of constant conflict between him and Jomo. Perhaps the conflict stems from the cultural difference between the Igbo and the Briton which Harrison tries to take up or construct for himself. He removes the insides of garden eggs and stuffs them with cheese and spice. Despite that, the guests, including Richard who brought them, could not eat them; they are not good enough. Through the contrastive marker, *but*, Odenigbo draws the attention of his guests to how Harrison's effort is nothing but a waste of garden eggs. Empirically, Odenigbo intimates how Europeans came to Africa and tried to replace African cultural values with European ones, i.e. by removing what is traditionally African and stuffing it with something alien. In other words, Odenigbo is saying that Africans and their cultural heritage should be appreciated for who and what they are. In the above interaction, we see how the meaning of race is not only defined, but also biologically constructed. The racial hostility between Africans and Europeans makes Richard, when alone in his apartment, to wonder why *the African and the European would always be irreconcilable* (Adichie 2007, 143).

It is interesting to see how Odenigbo presents himself as the sole authentic conveyor and protector of what is distinctly Igbo. This very act, enunciated through the rhetorical strategy — *what are these things?* — Odenigbo extrapolates the richness of Igbo food culture and downplays European food. The phrase *these things* is a condescending way of referring to what people eat. Yet again, Harrison's imitation of the British culinary technology which angers Odenigbo can be subsumed as a result of British domination of Nigeria and Africa by extension. This kind of discourse represents the complex nature of identity discourse emphasised in Chapter 1. We can hardly appreciate the factors, social, historical and cultural, that influence interpersonal connections because:

> Writing identity, as well as writing about identity, is a quintessentially modern predicament intertwined in the deliberate act of *writing* as *arriving* at a state of consciousness. The writing process, in itself, proffers a textual ordering of the world arranged according to an individual point of view (which by definition is selective) and displays a particular identity perspective. (Kavalski 2003, 1)

Odenigbo's linguistic choices are a mixture of cultures: Igbo and western. His adequate knowledge of both cultures becomes the platform on which he stands to oppose Harrison's ideas and British domination of Africa.

As much as one subscribes to the notion that race is 'biological' and cultural, as seen in the example sketched above, it is also socially constructed as the biological attribute can be dropped and a social identity constructed through the use of language. Richard is conscious of this — he drops his white biological identity and socially constructs an Igbo ethnic identity for himself: he learns and speaks Igbo. The meeting at the airport between Richard and Nnaemeka will suffice:

'You speak Igbo, sir?' There was a slender respect in the man's eyes now.

'*Nwanne di namba,*' Richard said, enigmatically, hoping that he had not mixed this up and that the proverb meant that one's brother could come from a different land.

'Eh! You speak! *Ina-asu Igbo!*' The young man took Richard's hand in his moist one and shook it warmly and started to talk about himself. His name was Nnaemeka. (Adichie 2007, 189)

Richard's use of language transposes the idea that language, not genetic configuration, is the basis of identification and acceptance. The heightened camaraderie between Richard and Nnaemaka is prompted by the latter getting to know that the former speaks Igbo. This makes Nnaemeka take Richard's hand. Taking Richard's hand symbolises acceptance, for in the Igbo culture, to shake someone's hand warmly is to accept the person. The Igbo proverb, 'when a hand shake goes beyond the elbow, it becomes something else', explains the premium the Igbo place on hand shakes. Interestingly, Richard himself uses an Igbo proverb to reconstruct the idea that colour is not a basis for racial differentiation or identification. In other words, Richard intimates to us that language is a significant factor in the social construction of identity. Throughout the novel, Richard's ability to speak Igbo paved the way for his acceptance among the Biafran people.

Richard's act of identity construction is an affirmation of Jaspal's views that 'The boundaries of linguistic identity are of course permeable; an individual may choose to leave their original group and gain membership of another by adopting a new language' (2009, 20). Identity discourse analysts who take up the social constructionism approach argue that language is a symbolic means of constructing an acceptable identity for oneself; this is regardless of whether the language is indigenous to the user or not. Language then is both a binding and dividing force.

Who has the right to name whom?

In the preceding sections, the focus was on the conflation of names and their ethnic symbolisms in Nigeria and, by extension, Africa, arguing that names are acts of ethnic/racial identity. In all, the emphasis has been on the importance people attach to names. It was also mentioned that naming is a system, not something that is done haphazardly. Since naming is a systematic process and having discussed how names can be used to provide information about the birth of a child or as a way of expressing personality/ego-boosting strategies and anti-ethnic/racial sentiments, it will be rewarding to bring this chapter to a close by drawing attention to a key factor in the Nigerian/African naming convention: the 'right' to name a child.

Why is it that it is a particular person who has the right to name a child? For an African, a name represents the bearer's identity and his or her 'voyage' through life. It follows naturally that if the wrong person names a child, the child's voyage through life is going to be turbulent. In most African communities, the naming process starts months before the child is born. The parents (generally the father, given the patriarchal order of most African communities) make a list of possible names. The final name to be given to a child is, however, determined by both the sex of the child and the prevailing circumstance at the time of birth, as has been already pointed out.

In the Bette-Bendi naming discourse, a child is named by the father. But where the father is absent, the grandfather does the naming. This practice is depicted in Betiang's *The Cradle*:

> He greeted the people — the elderly men and three women who had come to witness the naming ceremony. Outside, the villagers and unmarried women conversed in loud and wrangling tones under the natural sheds provided by the ageless mango trees…
>
> The old man began the rites which were short. He took the child outside the hut under the morning sun. He poured a little water on its head and placed a little pepper on its tongue. Back in the door way he held it in his arms and swung it to and fro, in and out of the open door with an accompanying incantation. The new baby boy was indeed being initiated into the many directions of its future engagements: the farm, the tapping forest and the many battles it would fight to justify its manhood. (Betiang 2011, 27–28)

This excerpt provides a detailed account of the ceremony that accompanies the naming of a child: *the morning sun, a little water on the baby's head, a little pepper on its tongue*, the symbolic to-and-fro swinging of the child in and out the open door and *an accompanying incantation*. In detailing this naming discourse, Betiang is invariably telling us that naming is not an ordinary exercise in the Bette-Bendi cultural philosophy. There is the Bette-Bendi saying that the child belongs to the mother only when it is in her womb but as soon as it is born, it ceases from being an individual's belonging and becomes a community property. This communal axiom is the reason members of the community are expected to be present at the naming ceremony. The presence of the community is quite representational: it means that the child is respected and accepted into its community.

The water on the baby's head symbolises peace and wellness; a little pepper on the tongue is to sharpen the child's oratory skills. The to-and-fro swinging in and out the open door carries the idea that the child will embark on several adventures and return home in peace; the accompanying incantation is done to ward off evil as well as speak positive things into the child's life. Expressions such as 'you will pick people's footfalls, but they will not pick yours' (you will defeat anyone who rises against you; no one will scuttle your progress in life) and 'you are a child who picks its share of meat from the midst of driver ants' (you are a strong person/warrior), among others, usually form parts of the incantation. The incantations are expected to see the child through the turbulent currents of life. The idea that life is for the brave at heart is always imprinted in the child's young spirit. This explains the fact that naming is an important aspect of the life of the Bette-Bendi people. This is not unconnected with the truism that naming provides opportunities for parents to positively influence the life of their children. There is a sense of reflexivity here: in invoking assistance and guidance for the child from the ancestors, the parents are also doing the same for themselves.

It appears that the function of the novelist's inclusion of the naming discourse is to reinforce or reinvent a way of life that is akin to that of the Bette-Bendi people that the advent of Christianity has almost obliterated. More importantly, it tells us when a child is named — shortly after its birth — and who actually names the child. Betiang's *The Cradle* gives us cultural insights into names and naming practices.

In *Yellow Sun* (Adichie 2007, 310), we are also introduced to a naming pattern. In contrast with the Bette-Bendi example, the naming of Baby is not done by parentage or by someone connected by blood to the child, but by one who is in-charge of the child's welfare. Mama's 'moral right' to name her son's child is contested because of her rejection of Baby. There is a transfer of the moral right to name a child from a blood relative to a willing care provider: Olanna. Even the child's father is excluded from the naming act. Though the pronoun, *we,* is used, it metadiscursively excludes Odenigbo and linguistically includes Kainene, Olanna's twin sister. It depicts fairness to Kainene and exclusiveness to Odenigbo and his family. Although the focus of this section is on who has the right to name a child, it does not seem to be beyond the purview of this book to mention that the naming of Baby follows the Catholic doctrine of christening. Christening, unlike naming, is imbued with Christian philosophy. It means the ceremony of baptism and also involves giving a child a name. This is why Father Damian will be informed and Kainene will be Baby's godmother. These practices of christening align with the Catholic doctrine of naming a child but differ considerably from traditional Nigerian practices.

Given the patriarchal system of many African families, the child's paternal grandparents supervise the naming ceremony. In the Igbo culture in which *Yellow Sun* is mostly located, naming ceremonies may take place four days after the birth of a child. However, whether a child will be named after four days depends on the health of the child's mother, since the mother is usually an active part of the naming ceremony. If her health is not good, the naming event could be delayed until she is strong enough to participate in the naming.

In Yoruba culture, just as it is with the Bette-Bendi and several other Nigerian subcultures, it is believed that the names given to children have profound consequences for the child. The profundity of the repercussions of a child's name leads the parents to begin making a list of the possible names the child will be given at birth. In *Difference*, Atta informs us of how parents begin to think of a child's name way before it is born and who has the right to name the child (Atta 2013, 217).

Known as *Isomoloruko*, the naming ceremony lasts several days on the last of which the child is named. If both grandparents are alive, the grandfather does the naming of the child. However, if the grandfather is deceased and the grandmother is still alive, she does the naming. If both grandparents are no longer alive, then either of the child's parents have the right to name the child. This is illustrated in Atta's *Difference* where Adewale and Deola's grandparents are dead, although Deola's mother is still alive. Therefore, the onus of naming their unborn child rests on them. It should however be noted that this naming practice varies from one Yoruba community to another. Although anyone could give a child a name, it is the name the child's father uses that automatically becomes the child's specific/personal name. This simply implies that it is the father who has the right to name his child.

All in all, the novelists' effort is to incarnate a practice known and revered by their people, a salient act of expressing ethnic values. It is useful to mention that these naming practices we find in the texts are not brought in by the novelists to fill some narrative space, but intentionally deployed to recreate an important index of their existence as a people — a way of connecting with their primeval selves in a fast mutating world. Despite the slight variation among subcultures, one thing is common: naming and its accompanying ceremony are an essential core of the African.

As I draw this chapter to a conclusion, it is necessary to note that in literary situations writers name characters and these names resonate with the characters' identity. This intersection is what makes fictionalised characters fit snugly into the subject matter of the story. Nigerian names, as noted at the beginning of this chapter, express something important about both the named one and the name giver. Nigerian writers, in their characterisation, transfer the Nigerian naming system into their creative works. It could thus be argued that there is a close connection between characters in the Nigerian novel and their names. In this chapter, I have discussed the interface of names and the enactment of ethnic identity, arguing that names and naming techniques can provide information about an individual's ethnic origin, can tell us of the circumstance that informs the birth of a child, can reveal anti-ethnic sentiments, and so on. In Chapter 3, I engage cultural identity construction.

3

Enacting cultural identity

The bond of language and culture

No study on cultural identity should overlook the intertwined bond between language and culture and how this interconnectedness serves as a vehicle for the expression and enactment of cultural identity. There have been numerous attempts by identity scholars over the decades to differentiate ethnic identity from cultural identity. While some scholars do not see any distinction between the two identity forms, others are of the view that both have converging as well as diverging points. In dealing with ethnic identity, many scholars such as Jaspal (2012), De Fina (2007) and Birnie-Smith (2015) believe that ethnic identity, apart from showing the link between language and a people, also explains the politicisation of language by an ethnic group with the motive of oppressing other ethnic groups. By one ethnic group displaying superiority over another, the latter is devalued in the process.

In the context of this book, I consider cultural identity as a critical portrayal of a people's ways of life that distinguishes them non-antagonistically from other people in relation to clothing/dress, food, endearment and familial relationship, among others, as mediated through the use of language. The implication is that cultural identity is universal 'because all people in the world are conscious of some sort of specificity that sets them apart from others' (Dorais 1995, 294).

It has been established that culture shapes the way people use language and language gives expression to peoples' values, beliefs and ways of doing things — in short, their culture. This suggests that there is an inseparable link between language and culture since language is fundamental to the expression of culture and cultural ways of doing things influence the use of language. Aspects of culture such as food, religion, familial ties, dress and even language are central to a people's existence and tend either to differentiate them or bring them together. Cultural values can bring people together, giving them an identity. That language functions as a vehicle for cultural identity expression as well as transmission is a well-known fact in linguistic anthropology.

The historical consequence of colonial rule is that English has been added to existing Nigerian languages. Nigeria is thus one of the most culturally and linguistically diverse countries in the world. Although studies have put the number of languages spoken in Nigerian between 150 and 450 (Ushie and Imbua 2011), the specific number of indigenous languages spoken in Nigeria remains unknown. Given the multiplicity of languages and the inability of the Nigerian state to work out a meta-language for its national integration, English has come to stay as the country's official language, and every Nigerian aspires to write and speak the English language. Nigerian novelists are conscious of this linguistic situation, and their use of language has shown the fundamental roles they play in preserving the languages of the various ethnic nationalities that were brought together for political reasons to form the Nigerian nation. Nigerian novelists' use of language suggests an understanding that the preservation of their cultural ethos and identity is significant to their existence. One of the linguistic vehicles deployed by the novelists under study in preserving and constructing cultural identity is the use of loanwords: these are the focus of this chapter.

Loanwords (or loaning) are not the only linguistic means by which cultural identity is enacted. But loanwords have underlying meanings; they transcend stylistic motivation to provide cultural information about a people. This is the reason this study is interested in loanwords. Loaning and borrowing are two linguistic notions that have been used interchangeably without paying close attention to the sharp distinction that exists between the two code-switching phenomena. Code-switching, a common feature of bilinguals and multilinguals, describes the simultaneous use of two or more languages in written and spoken situations. While a loanword, as described by *The Oxford Companion to the English Language*, refers to 'a word taken into one language from another' (1992, 623), borrowing goes far past taking an individual word to show the structural changes the borrowed words undergo as they leave one language to a host language. For instance, the word *oyinbos*– white person/people — as used in Atta's *Difference* (2013, 111) is an example of loaning. The word has been inflated for number, conforming to the morphological process of plural formation in English. This should ordinarily prompt a reader of the Nigerian novel to ask questions that transcend stylistic use of language to questions of why a writer would go through the process of localising words and expressions in the English language, especially when there are English equivalents.

Aside from preserving indigenous thoughts and providing equivalent terms to depict what they really want to communicate, Nigerian novelists loan indigenous expressions in order to provide cultural information about Nigerians and their contemporary ways of life. Through loanwords, the novelists aim at articulating multiple simultaneous Nigerian cultural identities in terms of food and food items, clothing/dress, dance and religious beliefs that portray the community-oriented life of the Nigerian people. In examining cultural identity in a culturally diverse country like Nigeria, analysts of the language of Nigerian novels are not oblivious to the fact that there are many cultures in the country. The implication is that they are, perhaps, aware that culture is not monolithic: it is a mix of different ways of doing things. Nonetheless, this study is not interested in the specificities that mark out one Nigerian sub-culture from another. Rather, the study is concerned with X-raying what is commonly shared among Nigerians and within Nigeria, things that are distinctively Nigerian, regardless of the Nigerian subculture from which the item is drawn. Table 3.1 provides quantitative information about the percentages of loaning in the texts.

Table 3.1 Indigenous cultural practices

Loan items	*Yellow Sun*	*Difference*	*The Cradle*
Food	59%	27%	14%
Dress	20%	47%	33%
Music/Dance	33.3%	33.3%	33.3%
Religion	25%	50%	25%
Total number of loanwords	137		

Table 3.1 is a presentation of the percentages of loanwords that provide information about certain cultural practices in the Nigerian context as captured by the novelists. The presentation of these ways of life by the novelists is to project the cultural identity of the Nigerian people as well as their contextualised literary significance. The table indicates that the highest percentage of loanwords denotes food, with 59% drawn from *Yellow Sun*, 27% from *Difference* and in third place, *The Cradle* with 14%. The sociolinguistic implication of *Yellow Sun* ranking higher than other two texts in terms of loan items describing food is not unconnected with the fact that the novel reflects the basic necessity of its temporal setting, war time. This setting may also explain why *Yellow Sun* ranks lowest, 20%, in relation to loanwords that designate dress. It suggests that during war people are mostly concerned with survival rather than aesthetics. For items reflecting dress, *Difference* ranks highest at 46.6% followed by *The Cradle* with 33.3%. When we subject a text to a critical reading, we can tell not just what words mean, but what they are *doing* in specific socio-discursive contexts. That *Difference* has the highest number of items referring to clothing is axiomatic. It depicts the Yoruba sentimental attachment to what is traditionally Yoruba, for almost all the items referring to dress are drawn from Yoruba. This is a tacit exemplification of cultural identity enactment. Although music/dance is the lowest at 33% in the entire loaning process, it does not suggest that dance/music is not an integral aspect

of the culture of the Nigerian people. It should also be noted that there is a decline in the liking for indigenous music/dance mostly in urban areas in Nigeria. Even when in some rural areas traditional dance/music still hardly take place, Nigerians who live in the urban area prefer 'contemporary' Nigerian music and dance — which is often a blend of modern hip hop and indigenous dance style. In contemporary Nigeria, the practice in which people assemble to sing and dance at night under moonlight is now not only almost non-existent, but also considered antediluvian in many Nigerian communities. Even when African dance and music are being reinvented in films, such as those produced in Nollywood, and in literary works, they are hardly practised in real life. Similarly, while 25% represents items that point to religious practices, they are used several times in the texts. For example, the word *dibia* occurs over 25 times in *Yellow Sun*, and *juju* about five times in *Difference*. If one were to account for them based on frequency of occurrence, they would have contested figures with loanwords describing food.

As noted earlier, attention has only been paid to items that are intrinsically Nigerian, implying that there are other linguistic items (for example, *jellof*, which originates from Wolof) in the texts that describe food, dance, etc. that are drawn from other world languages. Also, food, dance/music, clothing and religious practices have been concentrated on because they are the predominant items across the sampled texts. But more importantly, the percentage distribution shows the novelists' efforts at preserving their people's cultural ways of life in their creative writings. Therefore, these cultural practices are reinvented in such a way that these works function as the people's archive. Having accounted quantitatively for the occurrence of loanwords, I turn my focus to how they are used in the texts to enact or recreate cultural ways of living.

Loanwords describing food items

To see food beyond its nutritional value is to appreciate the fact that food is fundamental to cultural identity expression. Food provides pieces of information about who we are and where we come from. Montanari (2006) asserts that food is an indicator of cultural identity. For Montanari, food goes way beyond the biological need to survive to show the symbolic link between what people eat and their belief systems both culturally and otherwise. Our cultural inclinations have a way of shaping the choices we make about the food we eat as well as the codes with which we designate them. The implication is that food, like language and other identity building materials, provides information about how we perceive other people and these perceptions, in turn, shape how we relate with them. Almerico argues that the relationship between the foods people eat and how others perceive them and how they see themselves is remarkable (2014, 3). Evidently, change in food also points to change in cultural practices.

How then is food a linguistic issue? It has been briefly hinted that there is a link between language and the community which uses the language. Language and culture are remarkably entwined. For instance, lexical items designating food are culture-loaded which present definite information about a people. This suggests that our culinary habit is codified in the language system we use. The table below is a list of some common Nigerian food.

Table 3.2 Loanwords referring to food

S/N	Loanword	Meaning equivalent	Origin	Novel
1	*Garri*	Flakes made from cassava	Nigerian	*Yellow Sun* (324)
2	*Egusi*	A species of melon used for making soup	Igbo	*Difference* (2)
3	*Eba*	Solid starchy food made from *garri*	Yoruba	*Difference* (59)
4	*Edikangikong*	Soup made from fluted pumpkin	Efik	*Difference* (106)
5	*Moin-moin*	Steamed food made from beans	Nigerian	*Yellow Sun* (139)
6	*Arigbe*	Sweet-smelling vegetable	Igbo	*Yellow Sun* (28)
7	*Kuka*	A kind of black soup	Hausa	*Yellow Sun* (35)
8	*Akpu*	Solid food made from cassava	Igbo	*The Cradle* (18)
9	*Akara*	Fried bean cake	Hausa	*The Cradle* (55)
10	*Ugbamu*	A kind of black soup	Bette-Bendi	*The Cradle* (8)

One of the motivations for loaning words that describe food and food items is to preserve the culinary habit of the Nigerian people for whom the novelists traditionally write. In fact, a gloss over the above table indicates that the food and food items are traditionally Nigerian. The first loanword in the table, *garri*, flakes made from cassava through a vigorous process of fermentation and roasting, is a starchy-staple food in Nigeria. There are two basic ways in which *garri* is eaten in Nigeria. One, it can be soaked in cold water and eaten with any other food item like groundnut, fish (usually smoked fish) or coconut, or with a beverage, depending on the consumer's taste and economic strength. This method of eating *garri* — soaking — is very popular in many Nigerian communities. The second process is to make it into a paste by using hot or boiled water, depending on the starch content and the form the consumer wants it. The *garri* paste can be eaten with soup such as *egusi*, okra, *ogbono*, *afang*, etc.

Mainly produced for indigenous markets, *garri* is eaten by almost everyone in Nigeria. However, in certain quarters, *garri* is seen as food for the poor or those in extreme situations like war and famine. It is this view that underlies its adoption in *Yellow Sun*:

The antibiotics yellowed Baby's eyes. Her coughing got better, less chesty and less whistling, but her appetite disappeared. She pushed her *garri* around her plate and left her pap uneaten until it congealed in a waxy lump. Olanna spent most of the cash in the envelope and bought biscuits and toffees in shiny wrappers from a woman who traded behind enemy lines, but Baby only nibbled at them. She placed Baby on her lap and forced bits of mashed yam into her mouth, and when Baby choked and started to cry, Olanna, too, fought tears. (Adichie 2007, 324–325)

It is obvious that Baby is sick and has lost appetite due to illness. But an interesting feature of the above excerpt is that *garri* is the first food that is mentioned; all others came as luxurious food that will encourage Baby to eat. It was war time and *garri* was the commonest food anyone, even the poor, could afford. Beyond its use in the novel, it reveals that *garri* is relatively cheap and available all year round. It is not a seasonal food; it is also durable provided it is properly stored, keeping it away from the reach of water and a damp environment, for example.

The novelists' adoption of *garri* either in its raw or finished form — *eba* — repeatedly in all the novels is an indication that *garri* is a core Nigerian food item that expresses a Nigerian culinary identity. The conversation between a custom's official and a Nigerian lady at the Atlanta airport, United States of America, as depicted in the very beginning of Atta's *Difference,* is not only striking, but testifies that *garri* is a nationally recognised food:

'Any *garri* or *egusi*?' a customs official asks the woman playfully.
'No,' the woman replies, tucking her chain in, as if she is impressed by his pronunciation.
'*Odabo*,' the customs official says and she waves after he inspects her luggage.
The woman waves back. The camaraderie between them is tantamount to exchanging high fives ... (Atta 2013, 2)

One is likely interested in asking why the woman is impressed. The answer can hardly be distanced from the reality that she has been identified through something she holds dear, something that celebrates her as a person. This act of loaning is strategic: it makes it easier for the novelist to reconstruct a cultural practice that is known to Nigerians. Significantly, the author's use of the loaned item makes it possible for her readers to identify with her, to see her as theirs, since she tells their story.

Despite the fact that *garri* is very popular in Nigeria, in certain quarters it is seen as food for the lowly placed of society. For example, in *The Cradle, eba* prepared from *garri* is seen as food eaten by the domestically oppressed:

The crown witness told how Andoukye had boiled and eaten yam in the afternoon after preparing *eba* for them to eat; and how she had 'stolen' mother's groundnut oil from the chop-box. They had begged her to give them but she had refused and only gave a small piece to 'Mummy' who had cried — and would not stop. (Betiang 2011, 10)

Eba is represented as food for those who are maltreated perhaps because of its economical relativity and availability. But then, the various uses of *eba* by all the authors under this study indicate that, so long as the Nigerian culinary context is concerned, it is meant neither for the oppressed nor the poor but highly treasured in Nigeria. Also, in *Difference* we are told of the significance attached to *garri — eba*.

> Today, her *eba* and *efo* stew is delicious. After lunch, Lulu and Prof go upstairs to watch a DVD and she calls the house girl, Comfort, to get more water. (Atta 2013, 59)

The Bellos are not poor: at least they own a bank — Trust Bank. For them to eat *eba* and *efo* means that *garri* is well known in Nigeria: eaten both by the poor and the rich. In fact, it is the commonest food that can be found in almost every restaurant in Nigeria. It is expedient to state that in deploying these loanwords, these novelists have not only succeeded in making their story Nigerian, but also clarify that the adoption and adaptation of loanwords into their writings is a strategy of exposing to the world the food culture of their Nigerian people. Put differently, Atta could have used equivalent words in English to describe *garri* and *efo*, but she opts for the actual or indigenous names of the food items described because she is interested in celebrating her people's food culture. It is clear then that although language is not synonymous with culture, it certainly gives expression to culture.

Akpu is also another popular Nigerian food that is made from cassava: it is solid and rich in carbohydrate. Like *garri*, *akpu* goes through a vigorous process of preparation. The cassava has to be fermented for some days and when it is soft, it is sieved and the chaff thrown away. *Akpu*, also known as *fufu*, is much more popular in southern Nigerian than in the north. Moreover, in *The Cradle*, the novelist tells us that *akpu* is a core traditional food among his Bette-Bendi people:

> 'Have the children eaten?' Madam enquired perfunctorily. There was no need to ask, the clanging of pans and plates and the clamour from the kitchen said it all. The food was traditional two-course meal of *fufu* pounded from *akpu* and *ugbamu* soup. A kind of fast-soup made from some ground, powdery vegetable. Madam asked and Andoukye brought her a plate she always personally preserved inside her bedroom. It was the fried fresh fish she brought back from the market. Such was the occasional delicacy she allowed herself — and her husband. (Betiang 2011, 8)

Of course, it cannot be said that Betiang provides this kind of elaborate explanation for art's sake. The in-text translation tells it all: the author explains what *ugbamu* soup means: *A kind of fast-soup made from some ground, powdery vegetable*. This in-text translation delineates the narrative essence, i.e. why these authors loan indigenous words into their writing. The loaned items also depict the communal life of the people. It implies that dinner is a time members of a family come together to cement their oneness, their 'in-groupness'. The implication is that when *fufu* or *akpu* is mentioned, many Nigerians will know what is being described or referred to.

In a similar manner of cultural identity display as mediated through the loaning strategy, Adichie tells us how Ugwu, in a nostalgic throwback, narrates his people's food habit back home:

> His mother would be preparing the evening meal now, pounding *akpu* in the mortar, the pestle grasped tightly with both hands. Chioke, the junior wife, would be tending the pot of watery soup balanced on three stones over the fire. The children would have come from the stream … perhaps Anulika would be watching them … she would wait until the *akpu* was eaten and then divide the fish so that each child had a piece … (Adichie 2007, 18)

Although he is happy to be at Nsukka, Ugwu misses home; he feels detached from a way of life, something primal, some practice he was born into and grew up to cherish. Adichie does this narrative reversion to portray the food identity of her Igbo people of south-eastern Nigeria. The excerpt is quite informative. Just like the example lifted from *The Cradle*, *akpu* is taken during dinner. This details a similarity in the eating habit between the Bette-Bendi in south-south Nigeria and their neighbours in south-eastern Nigeria. Adichie's loaning technique, as does that of Betiang, accounts for how familial ties are strengthened by and woven around food. It is a polygamous family and through the linguistic means of loaning, the novelist presents to her readers how a polygamous family is knit together, everyone playing an integrative role in the survival of the collective. Importantly, Adichie's loaning practice communicates the idea that *akpu* is a core food that is eaten in Nigeria.

The food item *moin moin* is the occasion for another loaning procedure. *Moin moin*, also spelt *moi moi*, is very popular in Nigeria. It can be eaten alone or with other food like pap, custard, soaked *garri*, rice, fried plantain, among other suitable combinations. It is cooked either with leaves — its traditional method — or with foil paper. Even in the diaspora, *moin moin* is known as typically Nigerian. This conjecture is asserted in the example below:

> 'Adeola,' Subu's mother says. 'Is this you?'
> Subu's mother is frail with copper-colored skin. Her hands are arthritic. She hugs Deola and asks about her family and work. She has been steaming *moin-moin*. Subu begins to peel them out of wrapped foil paper.
> 'Come and eat,' Subu's mother says.
> 'Thank you, ma,' Deola says, though she is full. (Atta 2013, 219)

Deola and Subu are Nigerians who live in the UK and when Deola visits Subu, she finds out that Subu's mother came in from Nigeria. It is interesting to know that what she is steaming is *moin moin*. This loaning act is calculated in the sense that it reminds them of where they come from, that they are Nigerians who are used to a particular kind of food. It is important to note that these writers can still tell their story without necessarily loaning indigenous food items. But for them using these loanwords is an act of deliberate cultural identity construction. It suggests that they are proud of where they come from and their ways of life. Also worthy of note is that Subu's mother does not ask Deola if she will eat but asks her to *Come and eat*. In the traditional Nigerian life, one is considered uncultured and individualistic if one fails to give a visitor food. The worst of behaviour is to ask a visitor if they will eat. People are given food not asked if they will eat. So, the expression, come and eat, is an invitation that is not to be turned down. In fact, the ways these writers use the English language can hardly be differentiated from real-life situations in Nigeria. The Nigerian culture of inviting a visitor to the table rather than asking if the visitor will eat is portrayed in the above instance. In most rural areas in Nigeria, when people cook, they make provision for extra. The belief is that a visitor may come unannounced and the visitor must have something to eat. This aspect of culture is also manifest in the above example. Subu's mother does not mind if the *moin moin* was made only for her and her daughter; she must fulfil the cultural obligation of inviting Deola to the table. Subu's mother's behaviour is drawn from the cultural axiom that a host or hostess is expected to serve their visitor food.

Also, in *Yellow Sun*, we are told how the guests (mainly university academics) in Odenigbo's house prefer Ugwu's *moin moin* to Harrison's version of garden eggs:

> Even Ugwu looked amused as he came into the dining room to clear up.
> 'Mr. Richard, sah? I put the food in container for you?
> 'No, keep it or throw it away,' Richard said. He never took any leftover food back; what he took back to Harrison were the compliments from the guests about how pretty everything was, but he did not add that the guests then bypassed his canapés to eat Ugwu's pepper soup and *moi-moi* and chicken boiled in bitter herbs. (Adichie 2007, 139)

Another angle to this cultural representation is the fact that although *moin moin* requires a lot of patience to cook, it is something many look forward to eating. The above fragment also tells us the ways *moin moin* could be eaten; some use fish while others prefer hard-boiled egg and any other ingredient or method of their choice.

One thing is clear: the purpose of loaning *moin moin* is to bring to the readers' awareness a people's preference for something indigenous and to express a Nigerian sociocultural reality in terms of food. One would expect that some of the characters, as academics who have been exposed to Western ways of living (Olanna, for example, studied abroad),would opt for Harrison's canapés but instead they ignore them. It follows that we cannot understate the sociocultural relevance that informs the novelists' loaning act. The loaned words, besides preserving meaning, add value to the writers' creative efforts. This is compelling since it can be taken as a thoughtful celebration of what is typically Nigerian. Earlier, when Okeoma is surprised that Richard eats Nigerian food *so easily*, Odenigbo, boasting about his Nigerian food, remarks *Ha! I didn't think our pepper was made for your type, Richard* (Adichie 2007, 138). The deployment of the possessive *our* does not only set two cultures apart, but also indicates that many Nigerians do not have problem eating spicy food. The fact is that Odenigbo could have as well avoided the possessive marker; its insertion in the structure of the sentence is discursively calculated: it emblematically draws a distinction between 'we' and 'them'. The strategic use of language to mean in riveting ways has quite been emphasised in this book. Language and its use in the Nigerian novel should be critically examined, for there are layers of significations that are imbued in its literary use, especially in the use of loanwords.

A variant of *moin moin* is *akara*. While *moin moin* is steamed, *akara* is fried usually with red oil; it is more difficult to preserve than *moin moin*. It is also made from beans. Called *koose* in Hausa, *akara* is also known as bean cake in Nigerian English. Like *moin moin*, *akara* can be eaten at any time of the day. This is captured when Richard and Kainene where approaching Port Harcourt. Kainene asks the driver to

> 'Stop so that we can buy *akara* and fried fish,' Kainene said to the driver, and even the driver's stepping on the brake made Richard nervous. (Adichie 2007, 382)

The time of reference of the above occurrence is afternoon. However, the commonest periods *akara* can be found are in the morning and in the evening. One outstanding fact about the use of the loanword in the above context is that it explains how Richard easily adapts to life. Richard had left Susan in Lagos, a place where he did not eat *akara*, to live with Kainene. And as the war rages on, Richard sees himself as a member of Biafra, so whatever the people eat, he also eats. In so doing, he does not only win Kainene's love, but the people around see him as their own. As Kainene loans the word into English, it does not pose any semantic problem for Richard. We can therefore argue that through loaning of indigenous words and expressions, these Nigerian writers have achieved relevance and imprinted their cultural realities in their artwork. Put differently, without heavily modifying the grammatical structure of English, the linguistic means of loaning explicitly gives relevance to Nigeria's food culture.

But a symbolic feature of *akara*, like *moin moin*, is that it has no class distinction: it is food eaten both by the high and the low of society since virtually anyone can buy it. The fact that *akara* can be bought by anyone is depicted in:

'Did you lock it back?'

'Yes, I put back the key beside him.'

'Good boy, some *akara* money for you tomorrow.'

'What will you tell papa if he asks you?'

The boy remained silent, not really sure of what to say especially with the promise of *akara* money. (Betiang 2011, 55)

Although the use of *akara* in this context is conspiratorial, used as a bribe to lure Adie, Madam's son, to conspire against Unimke, it tells us two things: that *akara* has no class distinction and that it is every child's delight to have some money to buy *akara* at school during break period.But then, attention needs to be drawn to the sentential arrangement. The insertion of *akara* in the sentence, *Good boy, some akara money for you tomorrow*, does not distort the meaning of the sentence since *akara* only functions as an adjective in the context of use. Perhaps the author would have simply used 'snack money', but he opts for *akara* money. We should not understate the pragmatism that underlies this kind of functional language use. Like other novelists, it gives the author the opportunity to discuss what is inherently Nigerian.

Described by many from Cross River and Akwa Ibom States as king of soup, the loanword *edikanikong* is native to the Efik people of Cross River, Nigeria. The fact that *edikanikong* is native to the Calabar people and liked by many Nigerians can be inferred from Atta's *Difference*:

> Deola's father got along fine with Eno, even when Eno was just one of Lanre's girlfriends. He called her by her full name, Eno Obong. Lanre's other girlfriends didn't get more than 'How are you?' from him. After Eno and Lanre got married, he would tease her, 'When are you going to make *edikangikong* for me?' Eno would answer, 'I don't make *edikangikong*, Dad.' She called him Dad. 'Why not?' he would ask. 'Isn't that your specialty in Calabar?' 'My specialty is fish and chips,' she would say. 'Feesh and cheeps?' he would ask frowning.
>
> Eno humoured him on his birthday; her driver delivered a pot of *edikangikong*, which her cook had probably made. He danced around the dining table singing, 'Calabar woman, na so so powder, better go follow them, for God's power.' (Atta 2013, 106)

The general belief in Nigeria is that *edikangikong* soup is highly nutritious and so it is well regarded. The Efik people and some Nigerians are emotionally attached to the soup. *Edikangikong* is cooked primarily with a combination of two different vegetables: fluted pumpkin leaves (called *ugu* in Nigeria) and water leaves.

Perhaps it is necessary to mention that Deola's father preference for *edikangikong* to Eno's 'feesh and cheeps' is a demonstration of his penchant for what is indigenous. His dislike for what is not indigenous is manifested in the distorted pronunciation. Significantly, the loanword, *edikangikong*, highlights a distinction between the old generation and the new generation as represented by Deola's father and Eno respectively. While the new generation prefers what is western, the old stay with the indigenous. However, we see how the relationship between the two blossomed when she cooked a pot of *edikangikong* for him on his birthday. This loaning procedure is also pointing: it points to a particular set of people — the Efik people. But the loan item is used by a non-Efik novelist, Atta. This is a telling example of how, through loaning strategy, Nigerian novelists imprint a Nigerian identity in their writings. Loaning then is one of the major narrative techniques deployed by Nigerian novelists in the construction of cultural identity.

This narrative technique of loaning also reveals that food is a gate way to a man's heart. And Ugwu seems to authenticate this. He says:

> His grandmother had not needed to grow her favourite herb, *arigbe*, because it grew wild everywhere. She used to say that *arigbe* softened a man's heart. She was the second of three wives and did not have the special position that came with being the first or the last, so before she asked her husband for anything, she told Ugwu, she cooked him spicy yam porridge with *arigbe*. It had worked, always. Perhaps it would work with Master. (Adichie 2007, 27)

We are made to understand that some food can cause a man to do what he ordinarily would not do. So, when Ugwu burns Master's sock, he could think of nothing else but *arigbe*. His dependence on *arigbe* is based on his grandmother's cultural knowledge. He needs to do something to placate Master, so:

> He walked out of the compound, to the street, and looked through the plants …He had never smelt anything like the spicy sharpness of *arigbe* in the bland food Master brought back from the staff club; he would cook a stew with it, and offer Master some with rice, and afterwards plead with him.
> If the *arigbe* softened Master's heart, perhaps he could grow it and some other herbs in the backyard. (Adichie 2007, 28)

It can be inferred that food can bind up one person to another, i.e. food has the capacity to strengthen social bonds. Ugwu's story about his grandmother and his experimentation with *arigbe* imprints on the mind of his readers the idea that beyond the nutritional value we derive from food, food has the functional role of bringing people together. Similarly, one would begin to think that, given the bond between Ugwu and Master, (since Ugwu, unlike other house boys, is treated as a member of the family not a house boy) *arigbe* would have had the desired effect on Master.

There is a metadiscursive bond between the novelists' 'deliberate act' of loaning and the expression of cultural identity as it relates to food. This linguistic modality (the act of loaning) is an important index to the use of English in the Nigerian novel. Most probably, the novelists feel that if they provide translated forms of the words and expressions describing Nigerian food, the actual meaning of these words will be lost and the need to construct a Nigerian pattern of life will be defeated. No doubt, the food and food items discussed in this section of this book are among the ten top foods that are commonly grown and eaten in Nigeria. Importantly, the discussion sums up the idea that food, exotic ones, is a Nigerian way of life. Evidently, the novelists' deployment of loanwords referring to or describing food is an act of cultural identity display. These loanwords provide us with information about the food that is indigenous to Nigerians as well as Nigerians love for good, nutritious food. An interesting revelation is that Nigerians, apart from the vegetables in their soups (in Nigeria, we talk about soup in plural forms for there is okra soup, *equsi* soup, *efo* soup, etc.), rarely eat fruit. They prefer solid and starchy food. This is despite the fact that there are many different kinds of fruit that are grown in Nigeria. Moreover, Nigerians prefer what they call 'swallow' — *eba, fufu, amala*, etc. All in all, food is an inherent part of our cultural profile.

Loanwords referring to clothing

The conflation between clothing and cultural identity has long been explored by anthropologists. Therefore, this book borrows extensively from the anthropological sense of clothing as an aspect of material culture. While clothing as a form of material culture has enjoyed a harvest of robust scholarly interpretations, studies that have undertaken linguistic explication of the link between clothing and identity are still lacking. The focus of this section therefore is to account for how language, the use of loanwords to be specific, expresses the clothing or dress sense of Nigerians as reflected in the sampled texts. The basic concern is on clothing/dress, not on fashion. Although these two are often used interchangeably, they differ considerably from each other. While fashion simply describes changing trends which include, clothing/dress, clothing means 'the empirical/reality of dressed bodies' (Twigg 2009, 1).

Although the general perception is that dress or clothing (for the purpose of this study, cloth and dress will be used interchangeably) is not something that should ordinarily engage the attention of any 'serious-minded' scholar, what we wear remains a very important decision we take each day or each time we want to leave our house for our various daily activities. The overreaching idea that most often determines what we wear as we leave for the office, for example, is that our clothing must resonate with our profession. Obviously, this happens to almost everyone: the medical doctor must not forget their ward coat, for it tells them apart from the nurse; the banker must have a good relationship with jackets; the cook will not forget their apron and the list goes on. This suggests that what we wear 'provides one of the most ready means through which individuals can make expressive statements about their identities' (Bennett 2005, 96). When dress or clothing is mentioned, it should not be taken literally as what people wear to cover their body. Dress goes way beyond that. Dress is a cultural concept as it concerns itself with the way of life of a people. Our clothing enables us to virtually communicate who we are and where we come from to the world. What we wear or how we wear what we wear is an identity issue because clothing gives expressive force to who we are and what we want people to think we are or are not.

But then the question is in what way is clothing or dress related with language? Put another way, how is clothing a linguistic issue? Clothing is a form of non-verbal communication, a semiotic field of linguistic inquiry. Dress or dress culture, Olaoye (2013, 32) asserts, 'is a non-verbal communication system that is just like language system in the society'. He goes on to say that dress functions as paralanguage. Just as shabby or skimpy dress communicates penury, filthiness, etc., flamboyant dress conveys a message of wealth, power and opulence. 'Dress communicates a lot of things about the wearer, the on-lookers and the society at large' (2013, 39). Language does the same; it carries out these functions. Language is a means of communicating ideas; clothing communicates ideas too. Table 3.3 presents some loanwords that provide specific as well as contextualised information about Nigerian dress, their origin and meaning equivalent.

Table 3.3 Loanwords describing clothing

S/N	Loanword	Meaning equivalent	Origin	Novel
1	*Aliga*	Shirt	Bette-Bendi	*The Cradle* (93)
2	*Baba–Wondo*	Big trouser	Bette-Bendi	*The Cradle* (93)
3.	*Agbada*	Big flowing gown worn by men	Yoruba	*Yellow Sun* (48)
4	*Boubou*	Big flowing gown worn by women	Yoruba	*Difference* (57)
5	*Adire*	Dyed fabric made in southwest Nigeria	Yoruba	*Difference* (108)
6	*Asoebi*	Uniform worn by family members or well-wishers	Yoruba	*Difference* (105, 58)
7	*Ankara*	Cloth mostly worn in West Africa	Yoruba	*Difference* (78)
8	*Iro*	Wrapper	Yoruba	*Difference* (158)

Table 3.3 is an illustration of how loanwords are deployed by the novelists under study to describe the kinds of dress that is worn in Nigeria. The majority of them are indigenous; I have not discussed loan items of clothing that do not have a Nigerian origin. The reason for such exclusion is that they do not reflect Nigeria's typical way of life, in that they do not provide specific cultural information about Nigerians.

Apart from the fact that dress tells us about the wearer, it is also a symbol of solidarity and social identification, as in this passage from *Difference*:

> Aunty Bisi was busy distributing the *asoebi* and collecting payments. Another aunt accused her of having a profit motive. Someone else complained about the quality of the *asoebi*. Deola didn't want to wear *asoebi*, just as she didn't want to dance at her father's funeral reception. His funeral was communal, well beyond their control. (Atta 2013, 58)

From the point of view of cultural identity construction, these loanwords play an important role in the text. The loaned item, *aso ebi*, is a term with a Yoruba origin. It means uniform worn by family members and well-wishers to mark an event: it could be a birthday, a burial ceremony or a wedding event. In this instance, it is for a burial ceremony; the burial of Mr. Bello, Deola's father. In modern day Nigeria, *aso ebi* has become an integral semiotic component of many burial events, a cinematic explication of the Nigerian community spirit to be there for a community member in both cheerful and tearful moments.

Despite the fact that *aso ebi* has been constructed as a means of expressing solidarity, some scholars think differently. Nwafor, for example, believes that 'a stranger and an invited guest might seek recognition through *asoebi*' (2013, 2). Although *aso ebi* might be deployed to realise some ulterior motive, as some aunt accused Auntie Bisi, Nigerians do not primarily use *aso ebi* to seek attention, but to be part of the events of their community, to pass the virtual message that they share in the joy, sorrow, grief or any phase the community is passing through at a particular point in its history. The emergence and the popularisation of *aso ebi* as part of Nigeria's dress culture have seen the heightening of familial bonds as well as social connections as this excerpt from *Difference* makes clear:

> She backs into Brother Dotun, who flew in from Port Harcourt with Ivie's mother. In his *agbada* and cap, he looks like his mother, who is absent.
> 'Brother Dots.'
> 'Adeola-sco.'
> They shake hands. 'What's going on?' (Atta 2013, 108)

Although Dotun came for his father's burial, Deola easily identifies him because he is dressed in *agbada* and cap, the family's *aso ebi*. Obviously, the author, Atta, knows that merely providing the gloss of the above Yoruba words will not provide authentic information about the 'communal identity' of the Yoruba people. Thus, she loans these words directly into the structure of English to enable her to capture the sociocultural relevance of clothing for the Yoruba people at such events. In fact, Aboh writes that *aso ebi* 'which also graces an occasion, reenacts the communal ideology of the Nigerian people where communal imperative takes preeminence over individual ambitions' (2012b, 62–63). Though a word with Yoruba roots, *aso ebi* is commonly used in Nigeria and what it stands for is known by many Nigerian people.

Nwafor corroborates the foregoing, as he mentions that 'most people who participate in *aso ebi* in Nigeria have a common belief that they share a friendly solidarity' (2013, 6). It is therefore anti-familial, anti-community to refuse 'to adorn in *aso ebi* dress [as it will be] translated as dissent, questioning, and disagreement all of which are seen as tearing the "we" apart' (2013, 7). The morality of *aso ebi* is to keep 'we' intact and anyone whose attitude or behaviour tends towards 'tearing "we" apart' is considered an enemy of the collective. One does not have to be directly involved or related with someone for him or her to empathise or celebrate with another person. It follows, at least to a large extent, that rather than think of *aso ebi* as a construction of 'fake' oneness or 'we-ness', *aso ebi*, Aboh argues, 'dramatises numerous charitable acts that Nigerians do for each other without expectation of reward' (2012b, 63). What we can infer from the author's loaning of indigenous words is that the effect or essence of writing about her culture would not be felt in the absence of the indigenous words.

Besides the fact that dress functions as a means of expressing solidarity and oneness, clothing can, in many ways, also be used to identify a certain set of people among a particular community. Just as language can be deployed to impose a person's will over another, dress also serves as a vehicle of imposition. For example, in *Yellow Sun* and *The Cradle*, the loanword, *agbada*, is presented as the cloth worn by those who impose their will on others as well as by those who indulge in corrupt and criminal practices. This perception is captured in the example taken from *Yellow Sun*:

> 'Such a cool night,' Chief Okonji said behind her. Olanna turned around. She did not know when her parents and Kainene had gone inside. 'Yes,' she said. Chief Okonji stood in front of her. His *agbada* was embroidered with gold thread around the collar. She looked at his neck, settled into rolls of fat, and imagined him prying the folds apart as he bathed. ...
>
> 'I am not interested, Chief.'
>
> 'I just can't keep you out of my mind,' Chief Okonji said again.
>
> 'Look you don't have to work at the ministry. I can appoint you to a board, any board you want, and I will furnish a flat for you wherever you want'. (Adichie 2007, 48)

Agbada is a big flowing gown worn by men. Among the elite in Nigeria, it communicates power and affluence. It has become a dress worn by the politically and economically powerful. As presented in the above fragment, *agbada* is seen as a system with a malevolent identity. We see how Chief Okonji tries to impose his personality on Olanna. It appears that Adichie, in *Yellow Sun*, is telling us what men in *agbada* do to lure unsuspecting young ladies and how they defraud the government for personal gains. In this way, the loan item, *agbada*, functions as a linguistic code in which the novel sends messages about people of Chief Okonji's class or social group that corrupt the country and make young women their playthings. Betiang, also, provides photographic profile of men who wear *agbada*:

> The table between them was filled with drink and two plates of roast chicken. Unimke and Tarzan spoke in subdued tones at the same time eavesdropping on the noisy-couple seated next to them. Both wore white lace *agbada* with dog-eared caps. Unimke remembered his first night in town when he had met Alhaji in this very place. (Betiang 2011, 134)

Unimke and Tarzan are armed robbers. And, quite often, they drink at drinking spots where they can find what they like. Unimke remembers meeting with Alhaji in the same place he, Unimke, was drinking. Alhaji is the man who connected Unimke with a robbery gang. It is obvious that the drinking inn is a notorious place, a place where criminals meet. Although it has been argued that we cannot tell someone's intention by what they wear, the interactive situation can generate possible meanings. If meaning resides in context, it can be surmised that *agbada* embodies corruption; it is a form of dress with a popular culture of imposition and sharp practices as far as the Nigerian sociocultural matrix is concerned. We can, at least from the foregoing, say that the loanword is focalising because it isolates the addressees — those who wear *agbada* have criminal or questionable identity.

Iro, which translates as wrapper, is another example of a loanword that describes clothing or dress sense in Nigeria. *Iro* is commonly worn by women. Women, in Nigeria as women generally in other parts of the world, traditionally attire themselves in wrapper. This means that clothing is linked with gender. The distinction between what the sexes wear is seen here:

> Lanre describes Timi as his 'Attention Deficit Disorder Son.' They both keep close to him, wearing matching light blue *agbada*, and swagger as he does. Eno still has a serene air. She wears her white *iro* and *buba*, without a head tie. She has gained weight, but she is still a pretty woman. Her mother is in an *adire* dress and flat sandals and smiles at everyone, whether or not they acknowledge her. (Atta 2013, 108)

Culturally, there are clothes women wear and there are those worn by men. Clothing is thus one major way through which gender identity is visibly articulated. This is why, despite the influence of Westernisation and recently globalisation, some Nigerians still find it uncultured for women to wear trousers. Clothing then is a means of instantiating and enacting belonging to a particular gender or group. As presented in *Difference*, it is culturally abominable for a man to be seen in *iro* or *buba*, a variant of *agbada* worn by women, just as it is wrong for women to wear *agbada*. Clothing therefore embodies some gendered-cultural meanings. The loaned items are thus strategic to the enunciation of solidarity and oneness. By adopting these lexical items into the grammar of English, the author thus succeeds in drawing attention not only to the kind of dress that her people wear, but also to the difference in clothes worn by men and women.

So far, the discussion has been on clothing as a semiotic signification of cultural identity. The fact is however that dress can also function as a profound marker of national identity. In the example cited from *Difference*, we see the loan item, *adire*, a dyed fabric originating from south-west Nigeria. But it has become, like *agbada* and *asoebi*, a household name in Nigeria. Although it can be noted with certainty that specific dress forms originated from particular ethnic groups, 'identifying ethnic groups', argues Mbakogu, 'especially in the metropolitan areas, has become increasingly difficult, as there is high degree of homogeneity in the dress habits of the contemporary Nigerian' (2002, 129). This work upholds Mbakogu's views, and also adds that the increasing need to explore and demonstrate indigenous cultural heritage has made many Nigerians prefer the use of indigenous dress made from *adire* as a pattern of cultural representation as well as a way of preserving their clothing system in an increasingly mutating world. The consequence is that despite visible ethnic differences among Nigerians, there is 'greater acceptance of each other and a desire for further social integration and cultural integration' (2002, 129).

As exemplified in the sampled texts, gorgeous dress is an aspect of Nigerian's cultural identity. The appearance of loan items designating dress across the selected texts indicates that there is mutual intermingling of dress/clothing among Nigerians. It can consequently be inferred that the writers' adoption and adaptation of indigenous expressions referring to clothing items is informed by the value they attach to Nigerian cultural ways of dressing. These indigenous expressions are not brought into the narrative texture to fill in some space, but to invigorate a sense of identity. This is affirmed in real-life situations where the authors of *Yellow Sun* and *Difference* are often seen in Nigerian 'native' dress. Contrary to this being alarming, it reinforces their Nigerian-ness.

Loanwords describing dance/music and supernatural beliefs

Having explored in the foregoing sections how food and dress/clothing are material aspects of cultural identity in the selected novels, I now explore other aspects of cultural identity expression — dance and the belief in the supernatural — presented through strategic deployment of loanwords.

There is a dialectical relationship between dance and cultural identity. Just like other forms of cultural expression, dance reflects the community it emerges from. Dance, if critically examined, tells us stories about people, stories about their existence from the past to the present situations in which they find themselves. Scholars of dance and music hold the view that in most African cultures, dance (since it is difficult to discuss dance without making reference to music, the terms are used interchangeably) is an expression of the attitude, norms, values and spirituality of a particular culture. When people dance or sing, it is an expression of what is embedded in their ways of doing things and how they conceive of the world. In *The Cradle*, for example, there is the deliberate introduction of *Ikpatemana* thus:

> As the food and drinks disappeared into the vast tunnels of men, *Ikpatemana*, the all horn war dance group, took possession of the arena. The young girls sang and clapped as the animal-skinned masquerades danced in possessed frenzy. (Betiang 2011, 177)

The loanword, *Ikpatemana*, a war dance which, before the advent of Christianity and subsequent colonialism, was reserved exclusively for 'men.' To be given a 'manly' identity, a man was required to return from war with, at least, a human head. Invariably, the degree or extent of a man's manliness was calculated based on the number of human heads he brought back from war. But the colonial government, conscious of the fact that the dance encouraged tribal wars and killing of people, abolished *Ikpatemana*.

Yet, some things remain visibly striking: the *possessed frenzy* of the dancers and the instrument — *the horn* — communicate the idea that the dance still embodies its energetic war values and spirit. Moreover, the language of the music and the pattern of the dance are explications of the cultural values of the Bette-Bendi people. The use of the loanword seems to suggest that people continually live in and through their language; they even die in it. Through the technique of loaning words from his Bette-Bendi language, Betiang succeeds in telling us about the value the Bette-Bendi people attach to dance. *Ikpatemana* used to be a war dance. But today it has become a dance performed to mark events, to celebrate occasions. This is the reason it is performed to mark the return of prodigal Akomaye whose incestuous act with Adonukye kept him away from the community for several years. The subtext to the dance, in the context of the novel, is that he is forgiven and welcomed back to the fold. The dance term — *Ikpatemana* — therefore expresses the discursive function of identity. It means that Akomaye is welcome back to the community he belongs to. Then, we can surmise that the loaning of *Ikpatemana* functions discursively as it enables Betiang to talk about a communal way of reunion of his Bette-Bendi people. Perhaps it can be argued that no other lexical item would have explained the underlying cultural significance of dance to the Bette-Bendi than *Ikpatemana*.

Perhaps it is a universal fact that dance performs a dual role of cultural expression and entertainment. This assertion is very true of the Yoruba of south-western Nigeria. In *Difference*, Atta presents the Yoruba people's love for dance and music and the utilisation of dance as an avenue for social bonding and cultural expression:

> There is a Nigerian crowd in London that Deola is not part of. People who came in the nineties when the naira-to-pound exchange rate plunged. They came to work, not to study or get professional training. They settled in Lewisham, Peckham, Balham and any other '-ham' they could transform into a mini-Lagos. Through her church family, Subu gets invited to their *owambe* functions, where they dress up in *asoebi*, play juju music, spray money and eat *jellof* rice and fried goat meat. (Atta 2013, 23–24)

As discussed in the preceding sections, *aso ebi* is a cultural identity marker that tells a people apart from others. *Owambe* is Yoruba slang for out-door party that is characterised by dancing and singing. It is a common practice in Nigeria to find people singing and dancing as a pastime and as an avenue for social integration and connection. A close reading of *Difference* reveals some basic cultural requirements that grace *owambe*: *aso ebi*, *juju*, *jellof* rice and goat meat; all of these items, except *jellof*, are inherently Yoruba. In this way, although these characters live abroad, the chain of continuity between home and overseas is both sustained and reinvigorated. Besides enunciating the desire for the good life, *owambe* is a vehicle of social cohesion and cultural preservation. Despite being in the diaspora, these characters make the effort to provide the items that are required to make *owambe* as entertaining and pleasurable as it would have been in Lagos, Nigeria. In this way, loanwords are distinct lexical patterns which structure the cultural communicative intention of the novelists under the purview of this study. Moreover, the introduction of the loaned item asserts Yoruba identity as well as in-group solidarity. This can be seen in Deola's refusal to identify with the *owambe* group, which culminates in her distancing herself from her in-group and disregarding her cultural identity. Most importantly, however, is the fact that the author's use of the loanword tells us that some people exhibit their cultural traits when the need arises. Context, then, is crucial in helping readers to appreciate what writers mean when they use language. We can see how the contextualisation of *owambe* and other loanwords discussed in this study draw our attention to how identities are constructed, reconstructed, negotiated and renegotiated.

Dance gives joy. World over, it is observed that people dance to kill sorrow, to express joy and to connect with other people. Therefore, the adoption of *owambe* in the sentential structure of the novel is important in the sense that it portrays a cultural practice of dance as a core aspect of the existence of the Yoruba. *Owambe* brings members together, uniting them, enabling them to realise that they are integral parts of the community; that they have roles to play for the growth of the community. This agrees with the views of Onwueke, who asserts,

> Because traditional music is directly associated with traditional religious and

political system and preserved by culture, it generates social experience which goes deep and serves as link which binds each ethnic society; giving each individual that sense of belonging. (2009, 173)

However, people do not have a single identity; they have multiple identities that are constructed in line with context. Subu and her church members drop their religious identity to take up a Yoruba ethnic identity, indicating how multiple identities can be constructed.

I have discussed how loanwords provide cultural information about the essence of dance and music of a people. I now focus attention on loan items that explain the supernatural practices of Nigerians as glimpsed in the sampled novels. Religion has been variously defined by scholars in the field of religious studies. Religion and culture are related because '[o]ur cultural values often include particular religious beliefs, shape our way of living and acting in the world' (UNESCO 1999). Nigerians are religiously inclined in their thinking and consequently depend on the supernatural for solutions to invincible problems. Yet, the belief in the existence of a supernatural being and the manifestation of its power and control is not peculiar to Nigerians. In people's everyday existence, inexplicable things happen, things they cannot provide answers to, and so they are prodded to rely on an invisible being that has overwhelming power and control over the universe.

A critical engagement with the Nigerian novel published in an age of Christianity, modernisation and globalisation reveals that some Nigerians are inclined to a belief in a supernatural being. Like in the examples discussed above, through loaning, the novelists focused on in this book shed light on the religious practices of their people. For example, in *Yellow Sun*, Jomo, Richard's gardener, tells Richard about the power the *dibia* exerts:

> 'It's all right, Jomo. I don't want any of the fruit,' Richard said. 'By the way, would you know of any herbs for men? For men who have problems with … with being with a woman?'
> 'Yes, sah.' Jomo kept watering as if this was a question he heard every day.
> 'You know of some herbs for men?'
> 'Yes, sah.'
> Richard felt a triumphant leap in his stomach. 'I should like to see them, Jomo.'
> 'My brother get problem before because the first wife is not pregnant and the second wife is not pregnant. There is one leaf that the *dibia* give him and he begin to chew. Now he has pregnant the wives.'
> 'Oh. Very good. Could you get me this herb, Jomo?'
> Jomo stopped and looked at him, his wise, wizened face full of fond pity. 'It no work for white man, sah.'
> 'Oh, no. I want to write about it.'

> Jomo shook his head. 'You go to *dibia* and you chew it there in front of him. Not for writing, sah.' Jomo turned back to his watering, humming tunelessly. (Adichie 2007, 96–97)

Richard has an erectile dysfunction problem and he meets Jomo who tells him that the *dibia* can solve his problem. A *dibia* is an Igbo word for a medicine-man, herbalist or native doctor. In the Igbo narrative, as it is the case with many Nigerian subcultures, the *dibia* is seen as a link between the people and the gods. The loaning of *dibia* is a re-presentation of the Igbo ethno-religious ideology that a supernatural being exerts absolute control over the affairs of human beings. Jomo in a subtle manner tells us about the esteemed position of the *dibia* and the *dibia's* ability to turn impotent men into potent ones. It must be understood that it is not about a herb that makes a man gain his potency, but the ability of the *dibia* to know the right *leaf* to administer to his patient that made it possible for Jomo's brother to *pregnant his wives*. This is quite compelling because when people have issues, they turn to the *dibia* for solutions with the certainty that the *dibia* has an answer to their problem. This absolute confidence reposed in the *dibia* means that whatever problem the *dibia* is incapable of solving, the gods too cannot solve it. It follows that loaning is a linguistic phenomenon, a strategy of authenticating the spiritual identity of the Igbo of south-eastern Nigeria. It helps the novelist to bring her ethno-religious values to the forefront. This is linguistically compelling as Jomo relies on his Igbo spiritual identity to educate Richard about Igbo medicine.

In a symbolic veneration of the *dibia* as well as in expressing his religious values, Jomo clarifies to Richard that the potency of the herb the *dibia* administers, in the first instance, lies in the patient's direct contact with the *dibia*. In the second instance, the *dibia's* medicine is given to only his people not white Europeans and is not something to be written about. In so doing, Jomo ensures that his behaviour does align with the religious practice of his people. Adichie, in this way, is doubtlessly presenting in *Yellow Sun* the Igbo's unwavering belief in the supernatural. There are several instances in the novel in which the characters' existence is tied to the mediating role the *dibia* plays between the people and the gods. When, for instance, Odenigbo's mother is bent on sending Olanna out of her son's house because of Olanna's inability to have a child, Mama, it appears, knows the right thing to do and says:

> 'I will not let this witch control him. She will not succeed. I will consult the *dibia* Nwafor Agbada when I return home; the man's medicine is famous in our parts.'
>
> Ugwu stopped. He knew many stories of people who had used medicine from the *dibia*: the childless first wife who tied up the second wife's womb, the woman who made a neighbour's prosperous son go mad, the man who killed his brother because of land quarrel. Perhaps Master's mother would tie

up Olanna's womb or cripple her or, most frightening of all, kill her. (Adichie 2007, 126–127)

The clarification one gets from Ugwu's thought is that some *dibias* are more powerful than others. Mama's grouse is that Olanna has been with Odenigbo for some time and is yet to have a child. For Mama, it is not an ordinary thing for a man to continue to live with a woman who cannot have a child; her son must have been bewitched. So, Mama has to do something that will rescue her son from childlessness as well as to free him from the spell he has been entangled in. Critically, she is going to consult a more powerful medicine man who has the capacity to degrade Olanna's supposed charm.

Ugwu is gravely perturbed because he knows what a *dibia*, particularly the *dibia* Nwafor Agbada, is capable of. It seems that there is nothing Nwafor Agbada cannot do: Uguw has seen people go mad, rendered barren and killed. He fears for Olanna, and he is forced to go and see his Master in order to ensure that Mama is deterred from going to see the *dibia*. In another instance, Ugwu reports:

> She [Mama] unwrapped a small packet and sprinkled something into the soup bowl. Suspicion flared in Ugwu's mind; he remembered the black cat that appeared in the backyard after her last visit. And the packet was black, too, like the cat. (Adichie 2007, 260)

It appears the novelists under study are telling us that some Nigerians still believe that people can use substances (*juju*) obtained from medicine men to harm others. In some Nigerian cultures, various animals or their behaviour at certain periods of the day are often conceived as evil omens. Hence Ugwu's premonition that Mama is up to something evil is symbolically tied to the black cat. One might have the impression that the temporal setting of *Yellow Sun* covers the early 1960s and so such religious beliefs and practices are non-existent in the twenty-first century. Atta's *Difference*, published in 2013, a novel about 'contemporary' Nigeria indicates otherwise. Let us examine the exchange between Lanre and his wife, Eno:

> 'We were told they would cut off our heads and use for *juju*,' Lanre says.
> Timi holds his neck. 'Oh, Mummy, I feel sorry for you.'
> 'I was in England then,' Eno says, smiling. 'We didn't have *juju* over there.'
> 'Come on, clear off,' Lanre says. 'Calabar *juju* is the most potent.'
> 'We're talking about England now.'
> 'England has *juju*! What's the difference between psychics and *babalawo*?'
> (Atta 2013, 197)

If we set aside the argument between Lanre and his English-raised wife, and focus attention on the linguistic instantiation of religious beliefs, it is clear that the belief in the supernatural is still prevalent in Nigeria, justifying its portrayal in all the three novels under study. In this context, we should not downplay the fact that both Lanre and Eno have a university education. Their lexical choices are very important: it shows the investment they make in favour of their language. They loan *juju* and *babalawo* into their English sentences, implying that using the indigenous words will bring out the original meaning of the expression. A *babalawo* is the Yoruba equivalent of the Igbo *dibia*. Like the *dibia*, *babalawo* gives charm or *juju* to people who are in need of his services. Lanre, in a discursive move, draws Eno's attention to the fact that Calabar *juju* is the most potent *juju* in Nigeria.

This religious practice of seeking the help of a medicine man is also depicted in *The Cradle*:

> 'Now what is your problem?' Mallam asked the female prospect.
>
> 'Mallam,' the woman began. She told him how she had been married for three years and had never been pregnant for once. How at one occasion she had thought she was pregnant but some evil woman had melted the foetus and how she had bleeded the molten blood for three months. She also narrated the very many weird dreams and nightmares she experienced every night. Mallam Tanko then proceeded with his own interrogations, which as far as the woman is concerned sounded rather omniscient…
>
> Mallam Tanko prayed again for her and then made some razor incisions on the back of her hands and legs. He rubbed in some powdery medicament and dismissed her, asking her to be reporting every evening for seven days. Mallam Tanko went out with her into the dark night leaving Unimke in the charmed room. (Betiang 2011, 106)

Mallam is the Hausa equivalent of *dibia* and Yoruba *babalawo*. The woman's belief is that her inability to have children is nothing but the handiwork of her husband's other wife who has bewitched her. She therefore needs the help of Mallam to liberate her from the spell she is entangled in, believing that will make it possible for her to have children. Cognisant of the interplay between literature and real-life situations, it can be noted that the author's use of language is a representation of some Nigerians' religious identity. Mallam's act of rubbing some powdery substance on the woman's leg is similar to Mama rubbing some powdery medicament on Amala's back. This similarity in spiritual practices, as seen in Betiang's and Adichie's respective novels, informs the reader that there is some commonality Nigerians share in terms of religious practices.

My concern in this chapter has been the critical examination of loaning as a lexical strategy to construct cultural identity. We have seen how the authors in this study deployed loanwords as a means of establishing the authority of their indigenous languages as well as portraying the identity of the linguistic group to which they belong. This expression of belonging through loaning is a key feature of multilingual writers. By using loanwords to dissect the cultural exigencies of their people, the novelists are, telling us that their culture must be given expression in their creative works. And, in so doing, loaning from indigenous languages into English has helped them to showcase their culture to the world. Loaning is, thus, an important index of cultural identity construction. In the chapter that follows, I investigate the link between language and national identity construction.

4

Lexical and discursive construction of national identity

Language and nationhood

A few Nigerian academics and I were at the Greece Embassy in Nigeria for visas. But none of us was issued one. We were still in the vicinity of the embassy, expressing our anger at how we had left our respective, faraway universities for the country's capital, Abuja, only to be denied visas when two white men, who seemed to be angry over something, were dropped off by a car and yelled at the security officials to allow them access to the embassy. They said that they were Greeks, that their father was Greek and that they wanted to go home, and they needed visas right away. Listening to them, something interesting struck me: that although they no longer lived in Greece, just because their father was Greek and they had been born there, gave them the complete right to demand visas immediately. I was also fascinated by the two men's careful selection of pronouns in demonstrating their belonging to a nation, Greece.

Scholars in the field of identity discourse have argued that the concept of nation is inherently intractable in nature (Joseph 2004, De Cillia, Reisigl and Wodak 1999). These researchers are agreed that membership or belonging to a nation can be biologically linked, i.e. when an individual's identity is defined by their parents' birth-nation. Implicitly, by birth, one gains automatic citizenship of a country. This directs attention to the complex notion of nationhood or belonging to a nation. The desire, for instance, for parents to facilitate their children's American citizenship has seen many well-to-do African women going to the United States of America (USA) to give birth. The implication is that such children have dual citizenship – American and the country of their father's biological birth.

Another perspective to nation or nationhood is that a nation can be described based on its 'extended sense of an expanse of territory, its inhabitant and the government that rules them from a single, unified centre'. Since this sense of nationhood can be threatened by factors such as war and political influence from powerful nations, 'affirmation of belief in the nation-by-birth has been strongest' (Joseph 2004, 92). People owe their allegiance mostly to the nation of their biological roots. Going back to the sphere of the child whose parents are biologically Nigerians but was born in the USA, the child, if there happens to be any political crisis between Nigeria and USA, may line up behind his real country –Nigeria. If that happens, we can make a distinction between 'birthplace' and 'birth-nation'. Birth-nation or nation-by-birth (to borrow from Joseph 2004, 92) is biologically linked: it describes ancestral roots while birthplace is spatial: it denotes where one was born either by choice or by displacement. A Syrian child born in Turkey because of the civil carnage in Syria (at the time of writing) will grow up and perhaps some day say, 'I am originally from Syria'. We have heard immigrants use such expressions, and the majority of displaced immigrants have expressed the desire to return to where they originally came from. There is nothing complicated about where one comes from until one is challenged to prove it. Those who claim membership to a birthplace do so mostly for economic advantage or political stability which are absent or near absent in their birth-nation.

However, there seems to be some frontier that has been opened up in terms of identification. Individuals, who have dual citizenship owing to the distinctions drawn above, will find it difficult *expressing* their nationality if they do not speak the language of their birth-nation. If, for example, a Nigerian child was born in the USA and the child returns to Nigeria after several years, it will be difficult for the child, though Nigerians speak English, at least Nigerian English, to integrate and 'flow' with its people if it does not understand the Nigerian language the parents speak. That the said person, though owing to the fact that the parents are Nigerians, holds a Nigerian passport is not a guarantee for the child to be seen as a Nigerian. It follows that the sociological and political postulate of a person's national identity being tied to their holding a passport is punctured, as it has been demonstrated that language functions much more as a marker of national identity than holding a nation's passport (Suleiman 2006).

Despite Anderson's (1991) postulate that nations are 'imagined communities' because citizens of a nation do not know the majority of their fellow citizens and hardly meet one-on-one, many studies have shown that language plays an important role in constructing national identity. Although language is not synonymous with identity, language brings people together and gives them their distinctive identities (Bodomo and Teixeira-E-Silva 2012). People naturally bond more with those with whom they share a linguistic affinity. Language is thus significant to understanding how people negotiate or construct their national identity. Despite the fact that

Nigeria is an ethnically divided nation, and its citizens demonstrate loyalty to their ethnic group, many a Nigerian still expresses a belonging to a nation-state – Nigeria. Moreover, there are certain cultural and linguistic commonalities that are shared by Nigerians which mark them off or differentiate them from other countries, even within West Africa. Nigerian novelists are conscious of these linguistic and cultural commonalities, and they articulate this Nigerian-ness in their creative works.

I mentioned earlier that culture is an important index of national identity construction. Hall (1994) argued that the role culture plays in the construction of nations and national identities cannot be taken for granted. For him, nations are not only political formations, but 'systems of cultural representations' (1994, 200). In a cross-cultural and multilingual society like Nigeria, which comprises different ethnic groups, nation-building or national identity formation can only thrive through shared linguistic items that are common to members of the different ethnic groups, and using the shared linguistic similarity as 'the basis to try to bring these [diverse] people together to form a community, that is, a cohesive network of people constantly interacting with each other to advance their common interests' (Bodomo and Teixeira-E-Silva 2012, 75). Nigerian novelists are not only citizens by political configuration; it is ingrained in their metal architecture that they are Nigerians. Even Nigerian writers in the diaspora construct their Nigerian-ness through the use of linguistic items that are commonly shared by Nigerians. The point being stressed here is that cross-ethnic loaning and neologic practices –features of *Nigerianisms* and pronominal selections are both linguistic and discursive strategies that are deployed in the Nigerian novel to create as well as recreate national identity.

The ambivalence of expressing strong emotional attachment to ethnic origin while, at the same time, demonstrating a colossal sense of belonging to a nation state –Nigeria– is my focus in this chapter. The chapter reflects how language communicates a shared sense of Nigerian identity within situated interactional contexts. The pronominalisation of the self and the other, and the use of some linguistic expressions that are peculiarly Nigerian in interactive public spaces by fictionalised characters explain their being Nigerians. *Nigerian-ness* or demonstrating a belonging to Nigeria is premised or understood from linguistic similarities which Nigerians share as a people, and the conscious linguistic acts – pronominal strategies – which they utilise in interactive situations to display their belonging and not belonging to a nation. The novelists' representation of this linguistic modality of 'oneness' is a categorical construction of a national identity; this is despite the multiple ethnic groups and their sharp cultural and linguistic contradistinctions. To account for the confluence of discursive practices and extra-linguistic structures in terms of national identity construction, the various linguistic means and forms of realising a Nigerian national identity – *Nigerianisms*– and the discursive deployment of national pronouns are examined.

Nigerianisms

The general agreement in the Nigerian literary context is that there is one clear form of Nigerian English that is 'simply referred to as "Literary Nigerian English", the English that is of creative writing' (Adesanoye 2014, 46). Adesanoye's submission elaborates the on-going belief that Nigerian writers, right from the progenitors, have used English in their creative writing in such a way that one can point to a variety of English that is unmistakably different from Standard British English. What this signals is that the Nigerian literary environment exemplifies how English is adapting to sociocultural situations, depicting its various pragmatic uses and how the different contexts provide a framework for the propagation of a variety of English that many Nigerians can identify with, communicate through and express themselves in.

Soyinka, for instance, regarding the use of English in Nigeria's literary situation, believes that

> when we borrow an alien language to sculpt or paint in, we must begin by co-opting the entire properties in our matrix of thought and expression. We must stress such a language, stretch it, impact and compact it, fragment and reassemble it with no apology, as required to bear the burden of experiencing and of experiences, be such experiences formulated or not on the conceptual idiom of the language. (1988, 126)

Achebe had emphasised the above position and it has become a linguistic template which African writers have adopted for their creative exercise. Consequently, Achebeans and neo-Achebeans have made such a phenomenal success of 'bending' and 'stretching' the English language to establish a kind of English Adesanoye calls 'new English' (2014, 47) in their writings that making further comments on the matter in this study would be superfluous. There is however an angle to the literary use of English/language in the Nigerian novelistic tradition that is yet to draw the attention of critics. Even those whose attention has been drawn to the matrix of nuanced linguistic constructions are yet to argue beyond stylistic motivations to account for the discursive manifestations of language-in-use. The truth, as already pointed out in Chapter 1, is that way beyond styling their narratives, the Nigerian writers' use of language illustrates the link between language and identity –national– construction. This peculiar use of English that reflects the 'Nigerian-ness' of its users is known as Nigerianism.

Nigerianism, as used in this study, refers to those expressions that are used, shared and understood by Nigerians. It is a variety or manner of creatively using English to indicate the influence of indigenous cultures on the Standard British English. Nigerianism then describes a distinct way of using English that reflects the contact between Nigerian cultures, indigenous languages and English, giving it a local colour.

Describing the use of English in Nigeria in this way is only an amplification of the earlier views of Akindele and Adegbite that Nigerianism refers to '…certain linguistic features, which are specially related to some aspects of the Nigerian environment, culture or some indigenous languages' (1999, 64). Nigerianism describes the peculiar (not a substandard variety) use of English in Nigeria. The scholarly argument is that Nigerianism characteristically articulates the identity of its users. One outstanding aspect of Nigerianism is neologism/coinage. Jowitt has drawn the attention of his readers to 'one broad area of Nigerian English usage, that of lexis' (2014, 65). Needless to say, the English language in Nigeria has been undergoing 'domestication'. It appears natural for a study like this to focus on lexis because, even when at the levels of phonology and syntax Nigerianisms are evident, the lexis of any language is the 'block from which sentences are built' (Aboh 2014b, 171). Moreover, 'lexical Nigerianisms' are the most prominent in the sampled novels. Analysing Nigerian English lexis means identifying the various ways by which the lexis foregrounds the Nigerian-ness of its users.

Creating new words or extending/shifting the meaning base of pre-existing lexical items is a core Nigerian way of using English. Neologisms or coinages have been categorised into three: creations from existing stocks in English, loan adoption/ transfer from indigenous languages and those created from Nigeria's social-linguistic situation. The above-named categories are discussed presently.

Neologisms/Coinages from existing English words

Nigerians infuse existing English words with totally different meanings from the ordinary or denotative meaning of such words. While this is not an unusual way of using English, it reveals how such neologic practices fittingly capture the peculiar lifestyle of the Nigerian people. Table 4.1presents some of these words and their contextual meaning(s).

Table 4.1 English words but Nigerian meaning

S/N	Item	Contextual meaning	Source	Novel
1	Flashing	To beep someone's phone	Communication	*Difference* (93)
2	Uncle	Male sexual partner	Kinship	*Difference* (82)
3	Sugar daddies	Older married male sexual partner	Sex	*Yellow Sun* (339)
4	Area boy	Social miscreant/misfit	Society	*Difference* (26)
5	Mammy water	Mermaid	Myth	*The Cradle* (93)
6	Ghana Must Go	Bag	Corruption	*The Cradle* (126)

Almost all the items in Table 4.1 are found in the sampled novels. Even Nigerian novels that were not sampled for scrutiny in this study have evidence of these distinct ways of using English. For example, there is the use of *sugar daddy* in Ndibe's *Arrows of Rain*. Evidently, the lexical items in Table 4.1 are English words, except for *mammy*; but their meaning base have been shifted/extended to basically reflect the real-life situation in Nigeria. Except for *flashing*, which functions as a verb in its context of use, all the items in Table 4.1 refer to or describe people's identity and objects; that is, they function as nouns since they name people and things.

The sociolinguistic reality that events in society have a way of determining people's use of language practically applies to the Nigerian situation. We have seen how the advancement in information technology has introduced new words and expressions into the English language: *spam, email*, etc. are creative instances of how the advancement in information technology has added new words to the existing English lexicon. In some cases, existing words are given new meanings. The ordinary meaning is usually *abandoned* and the word gets an *appropriate meaning*, meaning that suitably describes the function the particular word is performing. An example of such a word in Nigeria is *flashing*, a word that came into existence following the emergence of the mobile telephone in Nigeria. *Flashing* is an English word that means 'the blinking of a light source such as light bulb or computer's cursor'. However, in Nigeria, it means an entirely different thing:

> 'Hello?'
> He sounds angry. 'Did you just call my number?'
> 'It's Adeola Bello.'
> 'Hey! You're in town?'
> 'Yes.'
> 'I thought someone was flashing me again.'
> 'Flashing?'
> 'You haven't heard of flashing? When you call, hang up and wait for a call back? (Atta 2013, 93–94)

As illustrated in the above fragment, *flashing* means a sudden and brief ringing of someone's mobile phone so that the person whose phone was *flashed* will call back. Therefore, in Nigeria, new words, which are variants of *flashing*, have emerged: *flasher* (noun) – someone who *flashes*; *flashed* (verb) – past tense of *flash*; and *flash* (noun) – the act of *flashing*. Contextually, Wale's phone rings and he thinks someone has *flashed* him. But Deola tells him that she is actually calling not *flashing*. Three things are worthy of explanation up to this point. One, Wale is based in Nigeria and is familiar with a communicative behaviour among Nigerians where someone can beep another person's phone, causing the person whose phone was beeped to call back. He also reveals that such an act can be annoying. Two, although Deola is Nigerian, she is based in London. And when Wale uses the Nigerian term, *flashing*, she does not understand what he means, the reason for her wondering what *flashing* means.

Because of the communication hitch, i.e. Deola's inability to understand what is meant by *flashing*, Wale is forced to explain. This implies that only Nigerians and non-Nigerians who have lived in Nigeria for some time can understand and relate to the coined item. Three and closely related to the second point is Deola's observation: *Not used that way it's OK*. Her differing with the explanation proffered by Wale is premised on the fact that she is looking at the meaning of *flashing* from its denotative meaning – what it signifies in terms of Standard British English. But Wale relies on the *appropriate* meaning, the Nigerian explanation and he expects her to follow in the conversation because she is Nigerian.

It is pertinent to reiterate that all over the world, existing words can be given new meaning, based on the communicative needs of a speech community, and membership of a community is often facilitated through the use of linguistic items which encode shared identity. In the Nigerian techno-linguistic context, the innovation, *flash*, is used to perform wide-ranging communicative functions: it is used to make someone call the *flasher*, to remind someone of something, among several other reasons, depending on the context from which the discourse participants are operating.

Another example in which an existing English word is semantically shifted, this time to reflect the socio-sexual life of the Nigerian people, is illustrated in:

> Ivie's Omorege was a victim of that. He met his wife, Patricia, when they were both students in university. They came from the same town in Bendel State. Patricia won a Miss Nigeria pageant. Her guardian was a family friend she called 'Uncle.' Uncle was a retired brigadier. He became a governor after military coup. He was ousted in a subsequent coup, but he made money while he was in office. He helped Patricia financially and bought her a car. He said he was taking interest in her studies. He turned out to be her sugar daddy. (Atta 2013, 82)

The English word, *uncle*, refers to a brother or brother-in-law of someone's parent. In Nigeria, however, the meaning of *uncle* semantically extends to describe someone's male extended family member, a child's teacher or any other elderly male member of a person's community. While this usage exemplifies the communal spirit of the Nigerian people as well as explicates the high premium of respect Nigerians place on elderly ones –by not calling elderly people by their name – the use of *uncle* also has a sinister undertone. As depicted in *Difference*, *uncle* functions as slang, a euphemistic way of describing an older male sexual partner who lavishes the younger female with money, outlandish gift items and material possessions like cars. This aptly describes the above textual extraction. We are told how Patricia, Omorege's wife, hides under the shadow of *uncle* to cheat on her husband.

A variant of *uncle*, though with a derogatory meta-discursive undertone, is *sugar daddy*. While *uncle* is used euphemistically, *sugar daddy* is often used dyphemistically to rail at men who indulge sexually with younger girls because of the material benefits they give such girls. Like other neologisms discussed here, *sugar daddy* appears in local newspapers. Just as in literary situations, the term is usually deployed with the negative connotation of undesirability. Such sexual relationships, despite Westernisation suffer inexplicable attack in contemporary Nigerian society. In *Yellow Sun*, just as with the example seen in *Difference*, Mrs. Moukelu's strategic language use accounts for the meaning of *sugar daddy*:

> Mrs. Moukelu finished a plait and patted Baby's hair. 'That his brother is a criminal. They say he gave army exemption passes to all his male relatives, everyone in his *umunna*. And you need to hear what he does with those young-young girls that crawl around looking for sugar daddies. They say he takes up five of them into his bedroom at the same time. *Tufia!* It is people like him who must be executed when the state of Biafra is fully established.' (Adichie 2007, 339)

Mrs. Moukelu tells Olanna that Special Julius, a contractor with the Biafran army, is a corrupt person who sleeps with young ladies. *Sugar daddies* just like the sex-related term, *uncle*, are rich and older married men who use their wealth as an advantage to sleep with young girls who are out for financial favour. *Sugar daddy* is used in Nigeria to frown at lopsided relationships, a vile situation where a man who is far older than the girl he has sexual relationship with. A female version of *sugar daddy* is *sugar mummy*. It describes older rich women who have sexual relationship with younger men because of the financial benefits the young men or boys, in some cases, get from the older women. Critically, the use of *sugar daddy* is couched in cultural morality. It is considered a despicable act for a man or woman who is older to be sexually involved with a younger person. Mrs. Moukelu's *Tufia*, an Igbo exclamation that rejects something awful or disgusting, acutely spells out her society's disdain for such a sexual practice, a practice that is alien to what she and her community hold sacred. On the other hand, it tells of how Nigerian society defines what is normal and what is abnormal in terms of sexual relationships between the sexes –that age is a principal determining factor in sexual relationships.

A linguistic item that requires explanation in relation to the neologic practices in the Nigerian sociolinguistic matrix is the use of *young young*, as can be seen in the above excerpt. Nigerians basically duplicate words for emphasis. There are expressions such as *small small* (too small) and *big big* (too big/quite big/huge), among others. Therefore, *young young* means a very young person. The discursive manoeuvre is that Special Julius is sexually involved with girls whom he ordinarily should not be. However, he does so because of the financial advantage he has over them. The examples sketched above suggests that, although native speakers generate new meaning from existing words, these new meanings cannot be found in native-speaker's contexts, the United Kingdom (UK), for example. If they are found in the UK, it must be in a Nigerian community or they are used by Nigerians who are based in the UK.

Overlapping with, yet clearly distinct from, the preceding examples is the creation, *area boy*:

> 'At Lagos State University. He was going there before he found his way here. He was not an *area boy*.'
> 'He wasn't?'
> 'At least that is what I was told. I'm glad he's made it, but he should stop telling lies about his background, and these *oyinbos* don't seem to be able to see through him.'
> 'Maybe they don't want to,' Deola says. (Atta 2013, 26)

This conversation characteristically exemplifies the patterns of speech one notices when Nigerians are interacting. The linguistic construction, particularly the lexical choices, demonstrates the manner Nigerians talk in real-life situation. *Area boy* is no longer a new entrant into the Nigerian linguistic space. It is used to describe hoodlums or social miscreants. Contextually, discussing Dara, a Nigerian musician based in London, Subu tells Deola that Dara is not an *area boy*. But perhaps the most striking aspect of Subu and Deola's conversational exchange is that when Subu uses the innovative term, Deola understands what it signifies. Both Subu and Deola had lived in Nigeria before relocating to the UK. Ideologically embedded in the discussants' lexical strategy is nationalistic oneness. Despite the fact that they are in the UK, language helps them to 'carry' their Nigerian-ness with them, an explicit instantiation of how language encodes identity. This stream of argument implies that if Dara, the subject matter, was present when Subu used the Nigerian expression, Dara would have understood her. But this does not apply to a Briton or a Londoner who has never been to or stayed in Nigeria, even though the term is English. In terms of identity construction, there is more to Subu's denying that Dara is an *area boy*. Her assertion that Dara is not an *area boy* is all about constructing a positive self-image for a citizen of her country. This is a typical identity construction that is hinged on an emotional display for the love of one's country.

The use of *area boy*, just as in the example of *uncle* and *sugar daddy*, epitomises the social-functionalist dimension of language and how it works in identity construction. The social-communicative situation in which people find themselves engineers them to develop new words that not only provide meaning to their existence but articulate to others who they really are. The various communicative purposes to which English is put in literary composition projects the idea that language is basically a form of psychological behaviour, playing significant roles in human thoughts and perception of reality. It follows that these neologic practices work contrary to the strong form of the Sapir-Whorf linguistic hypothesis: people are not prisoners of their own language. They are not essentially limited by language; rather, they employ language (as in the Nigerian example, 'bend' language) to say and 'do' things. The expression, *Ghana-Must-Go* is another expressive example of the interconnectedness between the use of language and the sociocultural existence of a people:

> Presently, a huge pot-bellied man carrying a Ghana-Must-Go bag entered and placed it before them.
> 'Please … spare my life.' The man spoke with a broken voice that seemed to be afraid of being heard, at the same time lifting up his fat arms in a gesture of surrender. (Betiang 2011, 125–126)

The use of *Ghana-Must-Go* authenticates the fact that people create language and the creative process resonates with their emotional state of being. It also implies that as language influences thinking, thinking influences language: a symbolic mutual interdependence. *Ghana-Must-Go* has a historical undertone. When the government of Nigeria deported Ghanaians in the early 1980s, it was the bag they used to pack their personal effects. But that meaning has long been dropped. It is now (*Ghana-Must-Gos*, plural form) a metaphor for poverty as well as corruption. As illustrated in Betiang's *The Cradle*, *Ghana-Must-Go* bag symptomises corruption. It is a bag those in authority use in pilfering money from government treasury. This is the plain meaning that is shared by many a Nigerian. This is why Nigerians speak of *Ghana-Must-Go politicians*, meaning that the majority of Nigerian politicians are rather interested in the money they make from politics than in their contribution to national development. But an interesting aspect of *Ghana-Must-Go* is the semantic change it has undergone: it is no longer a kind of bag Ghanaians used to put their things when they were deported from Nigeria, but a bag that those in government use in stealing Nigeria's public wealth.

Critically, the deployment of *Ghana-Must-Go*, just as have other coinages discussed above, shows how people's cultural ways of doing things influence their use of language in *experiencing* reality. In so doing, we use language to define our humanity as well as our identity. When *Ghana-Must-Go* is mentioned in any conversational situation, a Nigerian readily places it within situational constraints in order to know the appropriate meaning. The wide-ranging suggestion is that these lexical items insightfully depict how Nigeria's social-linguistic situation sets parameters for Nigerians' linguistic innovations, innovations that are determined by what they feel defines them in appropriate ways as Nigerians in relation to what they have experienced.

Loan transfer

Another way English has been indigenised to reflect the Nigerian identity is through the adoption and adaptation of loanwords from indigenous languages. In Chapter 3, attention was drawn to how loanwords are deployed to portray some cultural practices that are distinctively Nigerian. In this section, the focus is to highlight how Nigerian novelists loan words from diverse Nigerian languages in their communicative exchanges and the roles of these items in constructing Nigerian national identity. Table 4.2 presents some of the loan transfer that enriches Nigerians' communication, their meaning and their linguistic sources.

Table 4.2 Loan transfer

S/N	Item	Contextual meaning	Origin	Novel
1	*Oyinbo*	White person	Yoruba	*Difference* (43)
2	*Wahala*	Trouble/Problem	Hausa	*Difference* (121)
3	*Oya*	Go on/command	Yoruba	*Yellow Sun* (502)
4	*Oga*	Boss	Yoruba	*Yellow Sun* (54)
5	*Suya*	Barbeque	Hausa	*Difference* (137)
6	*Kai*	Exclamation	Hausa	*The Cradle* (93)
7	*Baba wando*	Big trouser	Hausa	*The Cradle* (159)
8	*Abi*	Right?/Isn't it?	Yoruba	*Yellow Sun* (165)

Loaning from different indigenous languages is a pervasive feature of Nigerians' use of language. This linguistic practice is replicated in Nigerian creative works. Though this act of cross-ethnic loaning is common with informal discourse, it does not suggest that identity is not or cannot be constructed in informal situations. In fact, identity scholars are of the opinion that it is in informal contexts such as online identity construction that 'real' rather than 'fake' identity is mostly constructed (Davies 2004).

Even a hasty glimpse at Table 4.2 indicates that the loaned items are mostly drawn from Yoruba and Hausa. This has both political and cultural underpinnings. Politically, the north, whose major language is Hausa, has ruled Nigeria for over thirty years of Nigeria's about fifty-five years of political independence, both under military regime and civilian rule. In the military barracks, for example, the lingua franca is Hausa, so the majority of the children who were born in Nigerian military barracks, regardless of their ethnic origin, speak Hausa. In fact, for many, Hausa is the first language they spoke. The reason for this is not too far to seek. The majority of Nigerian soldiers are northerners. This development is not unconnected with the Nigerian Civil War. Immediately after Nigeria's civil war in 1970, there was a recruitment strategy by the military that practically favoured northerners as well as southwesterners, the two large ethnic groups in the country, over Igbo and other minority groups. In a corollary, most Nigerian languages have enriched the lexicon of their grammar by loaning from Hausa, one of the earliest codified languages in Nigeria. This is the reason we find in Betiang's *The Cradle* items that are loaned from Hausa. Given this spread and the 'power' it wields, Hausa has no problem finding its way into the syntax of both indigenous Nigerian languages and English. Importantly, the cultural similarity Nigerians share makes it easy for Nigerian languages to take in words from other languages.

Yoruba's influence is in many ways attributed to two distinct yet interrelated matrices: the University of Ibadan and its literary tradition. Besides being the first indigenous university in Nigeria, the University of Ibadan had a literary club that birthed the progenitors of Nigerian literature in English expression. Moreover, many Nigerian writers, in one way or another, received formal training at Ibadan or were taught creative writing by academics who had studied at Ibadan. Perhaps it is the reason a former Nigerian President, Dr Goodluck Ebele Jonathan, at a graduation lecture at the University of Ibadan in 2012 mentioned that every educated Nigerian is a product of the University of Ibadan. Another obvious Yoruba influence is the concentration of publishing houses in Ibadan. Almost all the famous publishing houses are situated in Ibadan. It is just like media houses – the majority of Nigerian newspapers are situated in Ibadan and Lagos. The point being emphasised here is that Yoruba often finds its way into the lexical construction of Nigerians with no serious obstacle. This is also coupled with the fact that Yoruba has the highest number of educated people in Nigeria. Another factor that boosted the Yoruba profile was that alongside Hausa and Igbo it was considered Nigeria's national language – the failed WAZOBIA national language project.

That the words in Table 4.2 are mainly loaned from two Nigerian languages, Hausa and Yoruba, does not hinder mutual intelligibility among Nigerians as they are used in Nigerians' everyday conversational transactions. The item, *oyinbo* (*oyibo* for Igbo speakers and south-southern Nigerians) is a Yoruba word that describes a white person. The word appears several times in all the sampled texts either to describe a white person or a country. It is also used either as a noun or an adjective. In the example below, it is used as an adjective:

> 'Tell me, what has that poor woman and her four children got to do with whatever cartoon by one crazy Oyibo man?' (Betiang 2011, 166)

Oyibo functions as an adjective since it qualifies man. It is also spelled the Igbo way. Akomaye wonders why a cartoon in a faraway white man's country would provoke a religious violence in Nigeria. Akomaye discursively narrates how Nigeria is a country that is incessantly caught up in religious disturbances between Christians and Muslims. But, unfortunately, these religious crises always have ethnic watersheds. This is why most scholars are quick to conclude that any religious outburst in Nigeria has ethnic colouration. Mama Keke, a Yoruba woman, is killed in the riot and Akomaye marvels how she and her family have anything to do with the cartoon. Iyaji's answer, *They were on the wrong side of the mob: their names, religion and their tribe even*, sums up the nature and the dimension religious crises always take in Nigeria: the fact is that whenever there are problems in northern Nigeria, it is always seen as a clash between northerners and southerners. This is unarguably so because southerners who are Muslims are not spared by northern Muslims during such religious outbursts. In this case, religious identity is downplayed and ethnic/linguistic similarity or oneness sets parameters for identification and disidentification.

Symbolically and in terms of identity construction, the loaned item has a Nigerian identity:

> Tessa got curious about the word '*oyinbo*', having overheard other Nigerians using it and was awkward for Deola to confess it meant white, Westerner, Westernized, foreign. Tessa blushed. The British won't have any of that, stirring up stuff. (Atta 2013, 43)

The author of *Difference's* explanation is not only anthropological, but insightfully authenticates the fact that *oyinbo* is a Nigerian word that describes *white, Westerner, Westernized, foreign*. This implies that the expression is used to describe the 'other' and also a black or a Nigerian who desires to 'westernise' themselves. Attempts by some Nigerians to 'westernise' themselves are often rebuffed by others. In a thought-provoking narrative, Deola tells us how some Nigerian families are resented simply because they relegate their Nigerian-ness to the background and take up an *oyinbo* identity:

> Alero's family was the sort that gave Ikoyi a bad name. They were *oyinbo* to the core. Ikoyi people were not that *oyinbo*. It was too much work. They did not believe *oyinbos* are not worth emulating anyway; they only put on *oyinbo* airs to make other Nigerians feel inferior, shifting loyalties to cultures as easily as they changed clothes, unlike Alero's family who took things too seriously. Even her father did, which was unusual because no matter how *oyinbo* an Ikoyi family was, their father would let them down by saying, 'feesh and cheeps,' whipping out a cane to beat someone, or doing something else that would shatter the illusion and remind them where they were coming from. (Atta 2013, 111)

The passage shows that many a Nigerian wants to live an authentic life, a lifestyle that resonates with their cultural necessities. Evidently, in Ikoyi (a city in Lagos, Nigeria) people are content being Nigerian and will not expose themselves to the tedious job of being what they are not. This is also coupled by the fact that no matter how people try, they cannot brush off what they really are. The Nigerian proverb, 'no matter how it rains on the leopard, it cannot wash off its spots', echoes the sentiment that 'categories such as nationality, class, race, gender, etc. are taken as givens, in terms of which people's linguistic behaviour can be analysed' (Joseph 2004, 83). So, no matter how hard the Aleros try, their Nigerian phonological feature of pronouncing fish and chips as *feesh and cheeps* denies them the Westernised identity they strive to formulate for themselves. Though identity can be socially constructed, there are certain 'givens' that essentially tell us apart from others.

Another indigenous expression that has found its way into the lexicon of Nigerian English is *wahala*. *Wahala*, a Hausa expression for problem or trouble, does not need to be explained to any Nigerian whenever it is mentioned. Jaiye, Deola's younger sister, tells Deola about the arrival in Nigeria of some Chinese farmers who lost their land to the Zimbabwean leader's land policy. And Deola responds: 'So long as they do not bring their racial *wahala* here' (Atta 2013, 57). Deola's response, most probably, is informed by the racial segregation she has suffered in the UK. But perhaps the most interesting aspect of the conversation is that *wahala* does not need any explanation, despite the fact that the discussants are not all based in Nigeria. They understand what it means because they are Nigerians. This is even when the word has a Hausa etymology. Jaiye's question, 'What racial *wahala*?', does not mean that she misunderstands Deola, but that she wants to know the kind of racial *trouble* her sister is facing in the UK. Generally, *wahala* has a negative connotation.

It is expedient at this point to mention that despite the multiplicity of languages and cultures in Nigeria, there are some expressions that can be considered Nigerian. The role of Nigerian writers in trying to formulate a national identity is demonstrated in their act of loaning words from languages outside their own indigenous language. This is a telling ambivalence. Nigerian novelists are not just creative writers, but also 'creators' of a nation. They are consciously creating a Nigerian identity, and language is at the centre of such a 'creation'. The point is that for one to find these expressions as deployed in non-literary situations in literary situations as well, implies that the construction of a Nigerian identity is on the way.

Interestingly, this use of language suggests that a writer might be Yoruba or Hausa, but the novel must not be too Yoruba or too Hausa, for the Yoruba or Hausa novelist is not only Yoruba or Hausa but Nigerian as well. The Hausa writer, for example, is conscious of this matrix, of the fact that if their novel must be read by non-Hausa, it must be Nigerian. A novel can be Nigerian through thematic exploration and the use of language. Invariably, when Nigerian authors compose, they do so with the consciousness that they are composing for a Nigerian audience; they look out for those expressions that are commonly understood by Nigerians. One therefore can be informed about Nigeria by reading Nigerian novels. The following quotation tells us that many Nigerian intellectuals owe their allegiance to a nation – Nigeria:

> The driver stopped in front of her parents' walled compound in Ikoyi. He peered at the high gate. 'The minister they killed used to live around here, *abi*, aunty?' he asked. Olanna pretended not to have heard and instead said to Baby, 'Now, look what you did to your dress! Hurry inside so we can wash it off!' (Adichie 2007, 165)

Abi, a Yoruba word, could be used as a question or as discursive means of making a hearer confirm what a speaker said. The taxi driver who picked up Olanna, Arize and Baby from the airport does not use it exactly as a question, but to authenticate his supposition. The fact is that all Nigerians both literates and illiterates use the expression in their everyday conversation, regardless of their ethnic language. Another item worthy of attention is the expression, *aunty*. As it works in Nigeria, one does not have to be related to someone to be addressed respectfully through the use of a term of endearment such as 'aunty'. Such constructions of oneness not only draw from the cultural practice that elderly people or those who are socially above others are referred to by the use of endearment and respect-eliciting expressions. They also indicate that Africans see themselves as family of some sort.

Another expression that details Nigerian identity is the item *suya*; it is even used and understood by Nigerians in the diaspora:

> There are so many Nigerians here, more than there are in Willesden Green. It is almost like being back in Lagos. She passes Obalende Suya, a food spot she has heard about, and a row of yellow brick, semidated houses with 'For Sale' signs. (Atta 2013, 137)

Suya is an indigenous word for barbeque. Obalende is a suburb of Lagos, Nigeria. Of course, it will not come as a surprise if Deola stops over at Obalende Suya and finds some Nigerians who are there to partake of a national delicacy. It seems irrelevant to mention that Obalende Suya is mostly patronised by Nigerians, for it has a Nigerian emblem. As one reads Atta's use of language in constructing her Nigerian-ness (Obalende Suya), Anderson's idea that:

> [T]he nation …[as] an imagined community – and imagined as both inherently limited and sovereign, …imagined as a community, because regardless of the actual inequality that might prevail in each, the nation is always conceived as a deep, horizontal comradeship. (1991, 6–7)

clearly defines the pivotal rule of the Nigerian writer in national identity politics. Some Nigerian writers are based in the diaspora but their linguistic choices unmistakably carry their Nigerian-ness. This national retention which is evident in the use of language serves to reinforce the reality of being Nigerian, of belonging to a community – the Obalande Community. On Nigerian streets and drinking places, *suya* is found and it is mostly prepared by people from northern Nigeria. It is eaten by virtually every Nigerian, their social status notwithstanding. When Olanna left Odenigbo's house because his mother accused her of bewitching him, Odenigbo went to her flat with *suya* as a 'peace offering'. It appears that Odenigbo consciously does so because he knows that Olanna, like many other Nigerian women, appreciates it enormously when their husbands buy *suya* for them. Many Nigerian women consider a *suya* treat an interesting addition to their love affair. Although other animals are used in making *suya*, beef is the commonest. There are therefore various types of *suya* in Nigeria: *chiken suya*, *cow suya*, *goat suya* and *pig suya*. *Pig suya* is not very popular. Besides religious sentiments shared mostly by Muslims and some Christians, many Nigerians regards pigs as dirty animals.

The continuing argument of this study is that the analysis of the Nigerian novel in terms of language use implies an examination of how Nigerian society provides elaborate instances of its writers' construction or reproduction of what is essentially Nigerian. The supposition is that the business of the critic of the Nigerian novel should not be limited to the aesthetic use of language. An evaluation of the conjunction between the artistic qualities of the artwork and how well the literary piece has treated real-life issues or depicted people's existence is also important. The insistence on an approach beyond stylistic manifestations that looks more closely at how the novel X-rays the 'social-linguistic situation' in Nigeria does not entail undermining stylistic significance. Instead, it suggests that the essential core of a people always finds its way into virtually every literary tradition. In evaluating the form of the Nigerian novel, the critic does not need to underestimate the Nigerian-ness of the novel, for language can hardly be severed from the experiences it narrates as this study has so far revealed. This sociological postulate demonstrates how nationalistic sentiments and ideology interweave in literary composition. Put differently, the use of language – specifically the cross-ethnic loaning among Nigerian authors – can be seen as discourse strategies of constructing national identity, as well as other forms of identities. Of course, the idea put forward here is not that the Nigerian writer deals only with issues that are particularly Nigerian. A reading of the Nigerian novel shows that the writers are concerned with universal issues such as racism, terrorism and advancements in science and technology. This implies that the Nigerian novel can be subjected to universal critical standards. This is not the focus of the current study, though.

Having discussed how Nigerian authors adopt and adapt indigenous words to construct a nation, the focus is turned to those lexical items that are created within Nigeria's interactive space.

Creations from Nigerian linguistic space

There are certain lexical items that are frequently used in Nigeria which are not derived from English but from indigenous languages and others that have evolved as ad hoc expressions. These words have been so 'Nigerianised' that the ethnic language it emanates from can hardly be discerned. Some of these lexical items are presented in Table 4.3.

Table 4.3 Lexical creativity

S/N	Item	Contextual meaning	Linguistic source	Novel
1	*Inyanga*	Prideful attitude	Nigerian Pidgin	*The Cradle* (2)
2	*Lepa*	An attractive slim girl	Yoruba	*The Cradle* (6)
3	*Ikebe*	Female with big buttocks	Edo	*The Cradle* (71)
4	*Amebo*	Gossip/Gossiper	Yoruba	*The Cradle* (78)
5	*Mama Calabar*	Restaurant	TV Series ('Village Headmaster')	*Difference* (14)
6	*Naija*	Slang word for Nigeria	Nigerian Pidgin	*Difference* (25)
7	*419*	Fraud	Criminal code	*The Cradle* (115)
8	*Yab*	Mockery/gag	Nigerian Pidgin	*Difference* (114)

These expressions are mostly used as slang. Nigerian slang words are often loaned from Nigerian languages and Nigerian Pidgin English. Ononye and Aboh are of the view that 'slang terms in Nigeria lean heavily on Pidgin English and indigenous languages' (2010, 168). Both the slang drawn from Nigerian languages and that pidginised are widely understood by Nigerians.

In the multilingual Nigerian situation, Nigerian Pidgin (NP) – a language that combines English expressions with indigenous languages to form its vocabulary – is increasingly instituting itself as one of Nigeria's lingua francas. It is widely spoken in Nigeria by both literate and illiterate Nigerians. It functions effectively as a language of convenience because Nigeria is a country with many languages, each of which represents an ethnic nationality that contributes to the Nigerian nation. Since NP is primarily preceived as a language that belongs to all Nigerians, it bridges the communicative gap that exists among Nigerians of diverse ethnolinguistic affiliations. Even in northern Nigeria where Hausa is predominantly spoken as the lingua franca, NP is increasingly becoming an important lingua franca in the region. Furthermore, in the diaspora, NP is one of the linguistic means that Nigerians utilise to identify one another.

Although NP as a linguistic means of constructing a Nigerian identity is beyond the scope of this study, it is important to mention that many Nigerian writers, stretching all the way back to Achebe, have not only deployed NP in their creative works as a narrative technique, but also as a linguistic resource to provide their works with a Nigerian colouration and to enact the identities of their characters. In so doing, Nigerian writers illuminate the symbolic parallel between the use of NP and the formulation of a Nigerian identity. Even a cursory survey of Nigerian literature would illustrate this in terms of the cohesive role that NP plays in unifying Nigerians.

The expression *inyanga*, which means a show of one's self or a prideful movement, is widely understood by many a Nigerian. It is also spelt as *yanga* – pride/ego boosting. It is used to indicate the kind of 'showing off' both young boys and girls indulge in. Betiang affirms this assertion:

> For now and then – especially in the rains – a pot would overbalance a careless head of a girl in the youthful fit of prideful inyanga and fall off. And this was always followed by a cry of anticipation of punishment at home. (Betiang 2011, 2)

The Nigerian Pidgin term has underlying significations. It works well for the author's construction of village life. Betiang shows how an indigenous word like *inyanga* details the daily life of a Nigerian village. Importantly, *inyanga* reveals that villagers share a common tradition and a similar, if not the same, communal belief system, giving them a sense of belonging, a form of in-group identity. Obviously, the young boys and girls see one another as members of a particular community, and this calls for identification and solidarity.

Similarly, the slang word, *ikebe*, which describes a girl/woman with relatively large buttocks, is derived from the Edo language. Once the slangy term is mentioned, the image that comes to a Nigerian listener's mind is large female buttocks. This has a mental representation, as *ikebe* is drawn from the humorous Nigerian magazine called *Ikebe Super*. The magazine has a popular actress, Miss Pepeye, who has excessively protruding buttocks. Therefore, to *shake ikebe*, as used in *The Cradle*, is for a woman to show off her buttocks. Many Nigerian men, although they will not say so openly, prefer women with big buttocks to women with smaller ones. So, when Unimke, Betiang's protagonist, uses *ikebe* to address a lady, although intended to degrade the referent, he simply means that to *make ikebe* is to flaunt one's buttocks. *Ikebe* therefore does not signify all buttocks; only those that are relatively big. When Nigerians say, 'she get ikebe' (she has buttocks), they are simply referring to, as well as showing their appreciation of, a woman with large buttocks. But, more importantly, there is masculine objectification involved, since the concept of beauty or what a beautiful woman should look like is linked to her having *ikebe*. Furthermore, while the notion of *ikebe* is very popular among the elderly, the concept of beauty as articulated in the notion of *lepa* is for the youths, and maybe for those who are 'young at heart'. More significantly, the traditional Nigerian prefers the woman who has 'some flesh' to *lepa*, a slang used mainly by youths to describe a slim girl. And if this slim girl is beautiful, she is called *lepa shandy*. *Shandy* is a cocktail mixture which connotes something sweet. A *lepa shandy* is therefore a 'sweet, beautiful girl' both in terms of body image and sex.

Maybe it is germane to mention that an interesting finding is that language-in-use in the Nigerian novel depicts sociocultural features. Sometimes these expressions articulate the value system of the Nigerian people. The value system among Nigerians, where elderly people are expected to be respected, is depicted in:

> Jaiye raps, 'Don't even respect your ass, that's why it's time for the doctor to check your ass…'
> 'You shouldn't *yab* Funsho like that in front of your kids,' Deola says.
> Jaiye hisses. 'He's a fool. He'd better not piss me off today.'
> 'What did he do?'
> 'He has a girlfriend in South Africa.' (Atta 2013, 114)

Funsho is involved in extramarital sex and Jaiye resorts to *yabbing* him. Given the shared cultural background, Deola considers it completely inappropriate and ill-mannered for Jaiye to *yab* – make a jest of her husband – in front of her children. Deola fears that if Jaiye *yabs* her husband in front of her children, they will someday do the same to their father. Another angle to Deola's reprimanding Jaiye is that, as an elder sister, she has the moral right to scold her. In so doing, Deola imprints on Jaiye's mind the idea that verbal violence or violence of any kind cannot solve any problem. This is why Deola insists, 'you still shouldn't *yab* him in front of your kids'. The adverb, *still*, in conjunction with the compulsive modal, *shouldn't*, highlights the moral right Deola exercises over Jaiye.

Evident in the novelists' adoption and adaptation of everyday expressions into their novelistic discourse is the projection of their cultural ethos. These Nigerianisms give expression to experiences that are particularly Nigerian. The expression, Mama Calabar, a restaurant, as used in Atta's *Difference* points axiomatically to the Calabar people of southern Cross River State (see Chapter 3). They are known for their culinary expertise. The expression Mama Calabar has a mental representation that if one goes to the eatery, one will have the best of meals. It does not seem to be out of place to say that when one goes to Mama Calabar Restaurant, one will find many Nigerians who have gone there in search for something indigenous, some meal that reminds them of where they come from, Nigeria. Critically, the use of the expression carries the concept that the notion of belonging to a nation is not limited by geography: who we are can be psycho-linguistically represented.

In conjunction with the foregoing stream of argument, it is necessary to restate that the Nigerian is particularly involved in shaping, reproducing and constructing what is and what is not Nigerian. It is apparent that it is not only the European or the Westerner who has transferred their culture to Africa. The African writer is involved in the discourse of cultural transfer, a transfer of Nigeria's culinary habit to the UK, for example. This is so true. What this suggests is that understanding the Nigerian novel requires a critical examination of an interacting complexity of levels: the individual writer and the people's ethno-national consciousness. Questions such as how well does the use of language portray the national life of the Nigerian people? And to what extent has the Nigerian novel responded to ethnicity and its myriad of national problems? are naturally of interest to the discourse analyst. What does 419, for example, echo? What does it mean to the Nigerian? To answer this question, how it is used in the Nigerian novel can be seen in:

> Moses was something of an archetype of modern conman ship commonly known as 419. Being something of a juggler, people believed he could turn just anything into money. (Betiang 2011, 115)

419 is the Nigerian criminal legal code that penalises advance free fraud. Thus, the expression *419ner* designates someone who indulges in that kind of criminal or fraudulent activity.

The Nigerian novelists' use of language is no doubt an expression of their individuality. However, more importantly, it is a reflection of the linguistic situation in Nigeria which depicts, in a subtle manner, realistic linguistic verisimilitude. Put differently, language can point to the social status or identity of their characters. Some are monolingual while others are bilingual in their indigenous language and English; and yet others are multilingual as they can speak two or more Nigerian languages and English to some competent level. But perhaps the significant revelation of the use of language in the Nigerian novel is the articulation of oneness. The deployment of this linguistic 'oneness' is basically to project one Nigeria despite the multiplicity of ethnic groups and people's strong ethnic allegiance. It then follows that shared linguistic features and the ability to understand one another in interactive social contexts is a platform for the production of a common interest – Nigeria over ethnic loyalty. Even when there is a demonstration of strong emotional attachment to ethnic origin, Nigerians still display an immense sense of belonging to Nigeria, a psychological attachment to a nation. The next section is a further explication of how Nigerians, through pronominal strategies, express a belonging to their nation and an unbelonging to other nations.

Pronominal strategies

Another significant linguistic element that is often deployed in the construction of national identity is pronouns, particularly in narrative or conversational situations. 'Strategies', as used in this study, describes the conscious/discourse 'moves' that discourse participants make to enunciate their *belongingness* to a nation. These moves or linguistic expressions of belonging or unbelonging to a nation are often embedded in the mental frame of discourse participants which they play out as scripts.

Scholars who are interested in identity discourse argue that linguistic acts such as pronouns can be strategically deployed to formulate and establish a given national identity. Simpson and Mayr, for example, are of the view that 'the use of pronouns is an effective means of interpersonally representing in-and out-group status' (2010, 23). They argue that pronouns, apart from performing grammatical referential functions, include identity construction. The underlying message is that the preference for certain pronouns in interactive situations can reveal how people use language to align with a nation or orchestrate non-alignment with a nation. Corroborating this view, De Cillia, Reisigl and Wodak (1999, 160) suggest that the pronoun 'we' functions as 'components of constructive strategies (which) are persuasive linguistic devices which help invite identification and solidarity with the "we-group", which, however, simultaneously implies distancing from and marginalization of others'. In a similar view, Johnstone (2008, 156) posit that pronouns such "I", "you", "she", and so on represent the relationship of the self to others'. Our uses of pronouns in narratives or conservational situations represent the way in which we perceive the world differently from others based on our experiences. Yet, the choice of pronouns in narrating an individual's experience – personal identity – can only find expression in the collective. This is because personal experience can be correlated in so many ways with the collective – national identity, for example. The idea is that the personal only becomes meaningful within the collective. Johnstone's insistence that 'in highlighting what was important in their stories, narrators represent the experience of one's own life as a meaningful whole' (2008, 156) is an emphasis of the collectivist approach.

The above thought rhymes with constructionism where identity is seen as performance. The social constructionist paradigm highlights the linguistic means by which people tell us who they are or, more aptly, who they decide to be. A critical reading of pronominal selection demonstrates how identity is a discursive practice. The fact is that in interactional situations people construct, reconstruct as well as formulate who they are, and where they belong or come from. But then, identity, as already highlighted in the preceding chapters, can be assigned to an individual. An individual can be regarded as the 'other' by a discourse participant's preference for 'you', 'they', 'those' and other correlating adverbials that distance one from the other. Invariably, the identity individuals construct for themselves can be keenly contested or denied by another's experience of the world. In conjunction with the abovementioned, pronoun selection can serve various purposes and have wide-ranging effects. Strategic and conscious preference for one pronoun form, 'we' over 'I', for example, can be carefully planned and deployed by discourse participants to describe who they are or are not.

For the discourse analyst, therefore, pronominal reference goes beyond the creation of cohesion to include identity construction. The use of pronouns to create or reproduce national identities is evident in the sampled texts. This suggests the very complex nature of pronouns and what they signify in interactive situations, especially when the discourse is couched in conflict or ideologically contested situations. Pronouns, in collaboration with other linguistic elements, can provide information on how discourse participants project images of themselves in terms of nationalistic association. They are also capable of projecting a particular ideological orientation that influences the listener or reader's attitude. Pronouns, as deployed by literary discourse participants in the sampled texts, are explored from two dimensions: pronouns of solidarity/collectivity and pronouns of polarity and boundary mapping.

Expressing solidarity and collectivity

Pronouns are linguistic means of expressing solidarity and collective identity. The use of *we* in linguistically promoting national unity is shown in:

> 'So what was it the woman did to be burnt alive? I thought their problem was something else?' Akomaye wondered.
> 'They were on the wrong side of the mob: their names, religion and tribe even!'
> 'I wonder when we'll stop deceiving ourselves in this country. Some truths should be told. Tell me, what has that poor woman and her four children got to do with whatever cartoon by one crazy Oyibo man? What are the police doing?' (Betiang 2011, 166)

It is obvious that the *we* in the above fragment in union with the place adverbial, *in this country,* categorically refers to Nigerians and Nigeria. It is relevant to mention that Akomaye's concern is drawn from Nigeria's history of how religious crises continue to threaten the country's fragile peace. Nigeria as a country has a history of violent religious interludes which often leave hundreds of citizens dead and properties worth millions destroyed. Akomaye deploys the inclusive *we* to appeal to every Nigerian to set aside religious difference and embrace peace for the sake of country. The problematic religious narrative and the controversial or inadequate handling of such crises in the past have provided a fertile ground for frequent crises. This is the reason Akomaye asks, *What are the police doing?* This question is not merely rhetorical; it rather reveals Akomaye's desire for the security authorities of Nigeria to rise up to the task of providing security that is conducive to national integration and development. Interestingly, the active verb, *tell,* calls for reason. It charges Akomaye's listeners to set aside religious sentimentalism and promote national integration. In a tactical move, the pronoun, *me,* singles him out and captures his dissention with other Nigerians whose violent activities tend towards destroying their country.

The strategy of using the collective singular to enact national consciousness is a strategy that is often deployed by nationalists to demonstrate their *belongingness* to a nation. Deola illustrates this:

> Her tone is less casual as she tells him her family is in Lagos. As if to remind herself, she adds that her father's memorial is on Sunday.
> 'I'm lucky to be able to come home,' she says. 'Imagine trying to explain to an English boss the significance of a five-year memorial'.
> 'I know,' he says. 'My old man died in '86 and I was in the States.' (Atta 2013, 79)

In the above example, the singular inclusive pronoun *I* functions fundamentally to include every Nigerian. This is the reason it is strategically picked up by Wale. Contextually, Deola is happy that she will use the opportunity of working for LINK in Nigeria to attend her father's memorial. The fact is that, in Nigeria, a worker could apply for leave to attend a father's memorial. But this is an 'alien' practice in the UK where Deola works. Wale's response: *I know* denotes that he understands as well as shares in the cultural norm where the living honour the dead by being present at the dead's memorial. It is important to note that the cultural practice in some African communities is that one does not have to be related to the dead person to attend the memorial. Rather, there is an expectation for a member of the community to express solidarity with the bereaved. However, it is a grievous offence for a family member to absent themselves from a memorial.

Significantly, and in terms of national identity construction or reproduction, as in the above example, Deola emphasises the cultural difference between Nigerians and non-Nigerians with specific reference to the mutual relationship between the dead and the living. For Deola's English boss, a five-year memorial is insignificant. In spite of that, this *insignificance* becomes the platform for the articulation of 'we-ness', Nigerians who, entrenched in their mentality, is the unbreakable bond between the dead and the living. The culture of reverence for the dead does not only make them Nigerian but also reproduces a cultural practice that many Nigerians can relate with. Clearly expressed in Deola's pronominal choice is the fact that nationalistic consciousness emanates from a series of cultural beliefs that one holds about a nation. If Deola's identity enactment is interpreted based on the received tradition of national identity construction, the presence of the English Boss sustains boundaries of British-ness and their 'alien' culture informs her understanding and appreciation of Nigeria's cultural traits which underscore the notions of Nigerian-ness. This type of identification becomes for her a consistent process of coming to terms with who she actually is; it compels her to go home – *I'm lucky to be able to come home*.

Cultural 'sameness' or similarity that sets one nation apart from another, a basis for the formation of national identity, is the motivation for Deola's linguistic positioning:

'I want to be with a Nigerian.'
'Oh, don't be daft.'
'It's a preference.'
'Don't be daft, darling. Who ends up with her prince anyway?'
Deola gesticulates. 'It's all about…having a shared history.' (Atta 2013, 44)

Deola's level of education and exposure – that she studied in the UK and also works there – should naturally open her up to having relationship with any man from any nation. Yet, Deola's preference to be married to a Nigerian man, is prompted by the essential need to be connected with her roots. She goes on to categorically declare that the major reason she is inclined to marrying a Nigerian is *shared history*. The noun phrase reinforces Deola's perception of identity: the opinion that national identity can be calibrated along *shared history*. This *shared history* is a distinguishing feature, a way of life known and shared by a definite entity – *a Nigerian*. *A Nigerian* therefore symptomatically stands for any Nigerian who is not a Briton, for example. This Nigerian is mentally and culturally distinct from non-Nigerians. The *shared history*, which is all-encompassing – including social and ethnic symbols which also distinguish Nigerians from non-Nigerians – functions as Deola's argumentative anchor. Unarguably, her marital dream is nationalistic – to marry from a particular people is to belong to the people. The collective singular – *a Nigerian* – demonstrates an essence, a primordial proclivity to be with a Nigerian in every ramification of the word. In so saying, she becomes a nationalist who is determined to preserve her history. It appears that in defining herself within historical sameness, her identity is not coincidental but strategic so that her getting pregnant for Wale is a blessing in disguise. Her family's insistence that she comes home does not, perhaps, imply a negative attitude to Britain but a need to be with someone who will understand her. Similarly, it is this value for home and its cultural alignments that makes her to reject Bamidele's escapism. She urges him to return home: a place to which he fundamentally belongs. And when he refuses to do so, she considers him unpatriotic.

Cultural similarity and shared history conceived in this way, therefore, presents us with a curious concern about national identity and its construction. It suggests that shared history is a platform for solidarity and identification. This makes it easy for people to discursively project their belonging or alignment to a nation. Hence, Odenigbo's anger with a ticket seller is because he sees the ticket seller as someone whose act is equal to betraying his people's collective nationalism, the nationalism of being a brother's keeper:

'Let me help you here, sir,' the ticket seller said, in that comically contrived 'white' accent that uneducated people liked to put on.
Olanna was annoyed, but only mildly, because she knew the queue moved fast anyway. So she was surprised at the outburst that followed, from a man

wearing a brown safari suit and clutching a book: Odenigbo. He walked up to the front, escorted the white man back into the queue and then shouted at the ticket seller. 'You miserable ignoramus! You see a white person and he looks better than your own people? You must apologize to everybody in this queue! Right now!' (Adichie 2007, 43)

Odenigbo lashes at the ticket seller for degrading his people. Odenigbo's linguistic choices are systematic. The ticket seller has not only degraded *a people*, but his *own people*. The adjective, *own*, and the possessive pronoun, *your*, are linguistically calibrated, making the ticket seller's offence more grievous than it ordinarily would have been. Odenigbo's choice of the pronominal term and its adjectival counterpart is calculative: he could have only said *your people*. In this case, *own* strategically brings out the depth and magnitude of the ticket seller's offence against his own people. It can be said that it is the strategic deployment of the pronominal item and its correlating adjective that makes those in the queue cheer Odenigbo. But more pronounced is the distinction as well as differentiation that set nations apart from one another. *Your own people* – the referent group – is the group to which Odenigbo and the ticket seller fundamentally belong, setting them apart from the 'other' – *a white person*. Needless to say, Odenigbo's opposition to the subjugation of his own people is unmistakably nationalistic.

Another pronominal strategy deployed in perpetuating and constructing a national identity in an ethnically diverse country like Nigeria is the use of the plural possessive collective, *our*.

'Rex Lawson is a true Nigerian. He does not cleave to his Kalabari tribe; he sings in all our languages. That's original – and certainly reason to like him,' Miss Adebayo said. (Adichie 2007, 139–140)

As used in the above quotation, *our* expresses 'belongingness'. Nigeria has a history where many of its citizens are first aligned to their ethnic group and then to their nation of origin as can be seen in Professor Ezeka's response. Like in the example taken from *The Cradle*, Miss Adebayo, through extant nationalistic concepts, attempts to transform Professor Ezeka's 'ethnic thinking' to a national one – that one can only be originally Nigerian if one speaks some Nigerian languages. This is the motivation for her argument that Rex Lawson is a true Nigerian because *he sings in all our major languages*. By singing in *all our major languages*, the primary reason Miss Adebayo and Olanna like him, is an act in dismantling ethnic prejudice.

Metaphorically, Miss Adebayo imprints in the mind of her listeners that though Nigeria is a conglomeration of diverse ethnic groups as well as languages, Nigerians can still live together as a country. Therefore, 'cleaving' to a particular language is anti-nationalistic. Encapsulated in Miss Adebayo's proposition is the notion that the use of various Nigerian languages has the capacity of fostering national integration. Her choice of the inclusive possessive pronoun, *our*, is calculated: she establishes the idea that despite the different languages spoken in Nigeria, Nigeria is one and belongs to *all*. She distances herself from Odenigbo's reductionist marginality. As far as she is concerned, Odenigbo is an ethnic strategist who uses every opportunity to tear 'we' apart. It is this linguistic ideology that informs Olanna's longing:

> They spit the chewed cane out on the dust. Olanna sat with them [her uncle and auntie] for a while, but their Hausa was too swift, too difficult for to follow. She wished she were fluent in Hausa and Yoruba, like her uncle and aunt and cousin were, something she would gladly exchange her French and Latin for. (Adichie 2007, 57)

Of course, Hausa and Yoruba are among the three large Nigerian languages. In agreement with Miss Adabayo, Olanna constructs the idea that to be 'a true Nigerian' one has to be able to speak some Nigerian languages. She is so emotionally attached to Nigeria that she will readily trade her Latin and French for Nigerian languages, as it will make her more Nigerian than she is. Latin and French are languages that belong to other countries and do not carry the Nigerian identity she longs for. Therefore, Olanna systematically mediates an internal sense of belonging to Nigeria. It can be said that Olanna and Miss Adabayo's effort is to dissolve regionalism and encourage all to have a nationalistic outlook.

The pronoun, *we*, is the most complex among pronoun types. The meaning can only be understood when placed in its specific context of use. De Cillia, Reisigl and Wodak have shown how *we* distinguishes 'between an addressee-inclusive and addressee-exclusive "we"; and between a speaker-inclusive and speaker-exclusive "we"' (1999, 165). When Odenigbo uses *we*, he does not include every Nigerian, but makes reference to the diverse ethnic groups in Nigeria. He argues that *we* cannot pretend to be one Nigeria since *we* are different. Therefore, the use of *we* is exclusive since its deployment reinforces ethnic sentimentalism Nigerians like Miss Adebayo and Olanna are opposed to. Put another way, *we* refers to Hausa, Igbo, Yoruba, Tiv, Edo, Bette-Bendi or any other ethnic group, and that these groups should exist just as differently as they are rather than aspiring to being a united Nigeria.

Most significantly, both Odenigbo's and Miss Adebayo's brief overview of Nigeria's history provides the very broad historical and cultural spectra for the construction of what is Nigerian and what is not. Miss Adebayo's construction of a national identity is emotional because she insists that the recognition of as well as respect for other Nigerian languages and the people who speak them makes one an 'original Nigerian'. Her effort therefore is to disassemble ethnic sentiments and promote a national identity, just as Rex Lawson does with his songs.

It is this need for the promotion of a Nigerian identity that prompts Deola's response when Mrs. Nwachukwu asks her the ethnic group she belongs. Deola's tells her, 'I consider myself Nigerian and I hope we can be united in the face of this epidemic that threatens us' (Atta 2013,90). We can see how the strategic selection of pronouns co-indexes one another. The first person singular pronoun, *I*, is totally inclusive; it transforms from its singularity to include all Nigerians. In its context of use, 'I' amplifies Deola's projection of a national identity over ethnic one. We see how she shifts from the personal to the collective. The choice of the noun, *epidemic*, is also very striking. It indirectly refers to the ethnocentric disposition of some Nigerians, as represented by Mrs. Nwachukwu. For Deola, she does not see how the ethnic group she belongs to has something to do with her investigation. *Epidemic* is thus acerbic since it is capable of disintegrating the 'we-ness' Deola clamours for. In this sense, Deola presents Mrs. Nwachukuw as one of those Nigerians who are not dedicated to building a strong Nigeria. In fact, Deola's nationalistic initiative becomes even more tendentious by the incorporation of the rhetorical device, 'Does it matter?' Also, the question rebuffs 'ethnic-realisation' and promotes 'national-realisation'.

The above example illustrates how ethnic and national identities are co-constructed. The excerpt specifically shows a literary recreation of the existing conflict in Nigeria between those who think of themselves first as Nigerians and those who see themselves as belonging first to an ethnic group and then to a nation. Deola's, like Miss Adebayo's, linguistic strategies appeal to nationhood rather than ethnicity. Linguistic choices such as *hope, face, epidemic* and the strong verb, *threatens*, all collaborate to give force to her dislike of those who place ethnic sentiments above national ones. Thus, her indirect referential techniques, as in referring to ethnicity as an *epidemic*, entrenches her disdain for a practice that is threatening her country's national existence.

Polarity and boundary mapping

How discourse participants use language to articulate solidarity, to enact and formulate their belonging to a nation was discussed in the previous section. Just as people use language to express solidarity, they also use language to segregate, to polarise and to map boundaries. People differentiate and map boundaries on the basis of constructed identities. This is typified in the choice of pronouns as show in:

> 'So what's Biafra doing about oil now that they've lost the port?' the redhead asked.
> 'We are still extracting from some fields we control in Egbema,' Richard said, not bothering to explain where Egbema was. 'We move the crude to our refineries at night, in tankers with no headlights, to avoid the bombers.'
> 'You keep saying *we*,' the redhead said.

'Yes, I keep saying *we*.' Richard glanced at him. 'Have you been to Africa before?' (Adichie 2007, 448)

We, as used in the above quotation, is inclusive-exclusive. In the first instance, Richard uses the pronominal item to construct his belonging to Biafra. He politically sets aside his British identity and picks up the Biafran identity which is related to neither his birthplace nor his birth-nation. As can be seen in the above excerpt, Richard uses *we* repeatedly – three times – in an emphatic pattern to heighten his total solidarity with an emerging nation, Biafra. In this case, he sees himself as a part of a struggle a nation is going through, a struggle to liberate herself from the dominant 'other', Nigeria. Another interesting dimension to Richard's national identity formulation is the use of *our*. He could have said *the refineries*, but he opts for *our refineries*. This pronominal procedure expresses Richard's total identification with and belonging to the Biafran state as the possessive pronoun is categorically inclusive.

Symbolically and in a discursive move, Richard redefines the notion of nationhood: that belonging to a nation does not necessarily have to do with one's birthplace or birth-nation, but with one's voluntary identification with a nation's cause. This identity construction agrees with the social constructionist paradigm that 'identity is not something fixed and remains the same throughout a person's life. It is something that is constantly constructed and reconstructed as people interact with each other' (Paltridge 2006, 38). Strikingly, Richard uses *we* narratively to dismember himself from whites who profit from the Nigerian civil war. In so doing, Richard sees Charles the plump and Charles the redhead as dehumanised agents of economic oppression who take advantage of other nations. Though white, Richard, in a linguistic move, dissociates with the imperialist white. His question: *Have you been to Africa before?* is both antagonistic and *othering*, building on the emotion that Africa has been through a lot. What Africa has gone through becomes the building material for Richard's nationalistic affiliation to Biafra. Through the temporal juncture – *before* – Richard succeeds in painting a picture of two asymmetrical nations: the oppressed and the oppressor.

Cognisant of Richard's diplomatic use of *we*, the redhead does not hesitate to ask Richard the real meaning of *we*. Richard answers him politically. He brings in active political participation as a constitutive display of his belonging to Biafra. We should remember that he was with Suzan in Lagos and later moved to Nsukka, a Biafran territory where the struggle for a Biafran state received its academic momentum. Richard strengthens his argumentative micro-strategy by building on the memorial referent – *the bombers*. *The bombers* extend exophorically to the Nigerian government and its allies – the two Charles and many others – who are involved in killing his Biafran people. Richard's deployment of *we* clearly defines his national identity in terms of alienating himself from other whites and in terms of politico-cultural association. Richard's union with Kainene, from a core traditional Igbo practice, makes him Biafran. This is outside the fact that he speaks Igbo. The pronoun *you* also shows polarisation. *You* points to the antagonistic other and successfully 'maps' Richard away from the likes of Charles. Invariably, while Richard is Biafran, *you* – the Charles – are Nigerians.

In conflict situations, the activation of the second person pronoun, *you*, can work as a linguistic tool of boundary mapping, leading to ideological segregation among nations or races. This boundary mapping or demarcation strategy is activated by Deola's white ballet teacher:

> The first time she was ever aware her race mattered, she was in Nigeria. She was in primary school and must have been about eight. She was taking ballet classes at another school for expatriate children. The girls in the class were mostly English, but there were Chinese, Lebanese and Indian girls as well. Deola was one of a few Nigerian girls. The ballet teacher was English. She walked around clapping in time to the music, and ordering, 'Tuck your tails in,' as girls practiced plies. She would pass the Nigerian girls and say, 'I know it's hard for some of you'. She would pass the other girls and say, 'Good work!' (Atta 2013, 47)

You, as used by the English ballet teacher, maps a socio-psychological boundary, asymmetrically mapping out a mental boundary between nations and races: whites and blacks. Although the Lebanese and Indian girls are not whites, they are presented as better people and nearer to the British girls than the Nigerian ones. *You* therefore makes inferior and dehumanises the Nigerian, diminutively referring to the Nigerian as the weaker one. This is because other nationals are not told *it's hard for some of you*. The pronoun *you* and the qualifying adjective *some* are not only distancing and demeaning, but refer to a specific referent, the Nigerian girls. It thus trivialises the Nigerian girls' effort.

It should also be pointed out that the first-person pronoun *I* is widely inclusive; it covers all English nationals as well as their perception of Nigerians. The other girls are psychologically hyped. The phrasal element *Good work* highlights the positive values of non-Nigerians; yet, it significantly traumatises and mentally disparages the Nigerian girls who are discursively segregated by *I*. It then can be surmised that while other nations do 'good work', Nigeria does not. This kind of identity construction implies that who we are or are not can be constructed for us by others. Blommaert (2005, 205) puts this position concisely: 'a lot of what happens in the field of identity is done by others, not by oneself'.

The quotation below, as have the examples sketched above, exemplifies how national identity is discursively constructed:

'It is the Chinese I'm worried about', Lanre says. 'You know the Chinese. Before you know it, they take over your economy. Very soon they'll be telling America to shut up'.

'We're used to the Chinese', Deola says.

The spring roll was as Nigerian a snack as puff-puff.

'Hong Kong Chinese', Lanre says. 'These ones come from the Mainland and by the way, they hate each other'. (Atta 2013, 57)

Lanre's *I* is inclusive; the reason it is picked up by Deola's *we*. Deola and Lanre are two Nigerians who are discussing the influx of some white Zimbabwean farmers. And they are worried that other nationals will come and take over their country in terms of economy. The exchange between Deola and Lanre is highly polarising. The third person pronoun *they* is deployed to describe the Chinese as the antagonistic 'other'; people who specialise in taking over other countries' economies. The effective manipulation of the personal pronoun and the demonstrative adjective, *they* and *these* by Lanre aptly bring out the domineering disposition of the Chinese. With the strategic choice of pronouns, a form of nationalistic gap is mapped between Nigerians and Chinese and an ideological difference between them is drawn. Therefore, through the use of pronouns, not only can national identity be constructed, but nations' ideological differences can be discursively mapped out.

Similarly, Lanre's use of the explicit reference, *Hong Kong Chinese* and later the phrasal entity *These ones* creates a 'storied' discourse of antagonism or resistance since the Chinese is tactically tagged as the repressive *other*. Given this kind of mental representation, Lanre dissociates from the Chinese whose ideology is to oppress other nationals economically. The repetitive use of *they* to refer to the Chinese helps in consolidating Lanre's argumentative force. In this way, *they* performs dual discursive functions. One, it functions as an unbelonging/disidentification marker. Lanre and other Nigerians, as articulated in Deola's use of *we*, are ideologically distanced from repressive countries like China. The explicit referential mechanism – *the Chinese* – successfully paints them in negative light. Two, *they* implicitly refers to the economic ideology of China. Perhaps the fact that China is competing favourably with America and is amongst the biggest economies in the world is no news. Yet, that is not what Lanre draws attention to; he is rather worried by the manner *they* take over other countries' economies. The temporal referential tool – *Very soon* – captures Lanre's resentment with how quickly and the vulgarity with which the Chinese economically suppress other nations of the world: *they'll be telling America to shut up*. There is therefore explicit linguistic reflexivity between pronominal selection and national identity construction through alignment and disaffiliating patterns.

In a related manner, Olanna, while breaking up with Mohammed her Hausa lover, narrates her difference from whites whose behaviour is antithetical to her primal cultural pattern:

> 'I am not like white people,' she said quietly.
> Mohammed glanced at her. 'Of course, you're a nationalist and a patriot,
> and soon you will marry your lecturer the freedom fighter.' (Adichie 2007, 64)

Mohammed's response is not derisive, as it appears, but an affirmation of Olanna's nationalistic ideology, a political behaviour evidently different from white people. After studying abroad and given her parentage, Olanna could have stayed back in the diaspora, but her nationalistic patriotism encourages her to return to Nigeria and take up a lecturing position. Of course, this is a wakeup call to all to return home and make their country a better place. Her preference for a lecturer lover and a lecturing job all point to the fact that lecturing will give her the opportunity to serve her country and educate her people; the reason she prefers a lecturing job to the ministry position Chief Okonji offered her.

The analysis shows that pronouns are linguistic strategies discourse participants deploy to linguistically indicate either belonging to a nation or not belonging to it. It has been pointed out that the kind of relationship established between the way writers use language and the situation they describe is a pointer to the way texts work in reproducing identities. Literary texts can therefore 'present a miscellany of patterns of pronominal reference that say much about social relationships' (Aboh 2013a, 172). The pronominal selection demonstrates a discursive technique that depicts the novelists' conscious and ideological construction of a national identity. In reading the novels under study, it is soon discovered that the writers' use of language can hardly be divulged from the social realities of their immediate Nigerian society. The various excerpts analysed above show identity as something that is performed, constructed, formulated and reconstructed. In this way, identity is not fixed since it can be historically constructed in interaction and can also be conflictual.

This chapter explored the intersection of language and the construction of national identity. In exploring the complex notion of national identity construction, linguistic items such as Nigerianisms (loan transfer, neologism and lexical creativity) and pronominalisation techniques were critically examined. These are linguistic and discursive strategies that are deployed in the Nigerian novel to create and recreate national identity. Such linguistic investigation indicates that the Nigerian novel provides space for enunciating national identity or identities. There is also an intersection between the use of language and the construction of gender identities: this is the fulcrum of the next chapter.

5

Language as a marker of gender identity

The juncture of language and gender

Existing studies on gender identity using the Nigerian novel as a point of reference have demonstrated how gender identities are profoundly textualised. However, the majority of these studies depict an apparent imbalance in their presentations of gendered identities. The prevailing conclusion is that men in conjunction with society collaborate to dominate women. Fonchingong, for instance, has drawn attention to how 'Contemporary female writers have made giant strides in an attempt to re-define and focalize on the one-sided presentation of the African woman in the African novel' (2006, 142). Similarly, in her comparative study of Chinua Achebe's *Things Fall Apart* and Akachi Adimora-Ezeigbo's *The Last of the Strong Ones*, Okereke (2014) highlights the disordered and biased presentation of women by male writers. Okereke's summation, like some female critics, seems to imply that the primary business of any female writer is to re-organise the world in a way that both men and women will be treated equally.

Ladele's views about male-female intersection are not different from those of Okereke and Fonchingong:

> In African literature today, including that of Nigeria, there seems to be an identity crisis for women as we perceive a disjuncture between the typical portrayal of women especially in male-authored literatures as weak and inconsequential in the scheme of things and the current emergence of a new breed of women from all over the continent. (2009, 70)

The feminist movement (Butler 1990; Jack 1991; Mills 1995) has articulated this view well enough in various forms of writings and debates. But we need to examine carefully its finer influences. In other words, we need a close, empirical and detailed analysis of language and its co-construction of gender and identity. Moreover,

Ladele's sweeping and partisan assertion does not only 'disjuncture', to borrow her own word, objective criticism, but is also unjustifiable as it undermines the nuanced way both males and females use language to dominate each other and the positive portrayal of female characters by male authors. There are many African male writers who have through the use of language written women into metaphysical significance. In Betiang's *The Cradle*, for example, we see how Andoukye, a female character, is projected as a symbol of humility, one whose virtue of calm perseverance serves as the epicentre of human morality and an embodiment of human continuity. Betiang's construction of Andoukye's identity reveals how he is totally against male subjugation of females, illuminating how a male author can be a 'feminist at heart'.

The inference that can be drawn from the above argument is that there is a lingering silence — the majority of studies on gender identities has not shown how a woman can also be the architect of her own problems. This study shows that women sometimes play dominant roles in the debasement of other women. However, Orchardson-Mazrui (2006) believes that the way men use language clearly devalues women. While Orchardson-Mazrui's argument is to an extent a fact, it does not apply to every situational use of language since both sexes use language metadiscursively to degrade each other.

The common idea therefore behind feminist studies from disciplines within and outside the humanities is that society generally treats men better than women; thus, society makes man the superior being. Scholars such as Odi (2013) have linked such dominance to the biblical account of how Adam was the first to be created. Such a creation story, argues Odi, naturally puts the woman in a subdued position in society. In the light of this, many feminist theorists have argued that the woman is always the victim of oppression by man in the way language is used. Scholars who have followed this path to gender studies are of the view that the analysis of linguistic acts is a core phenomenon of human relationships. For these scholars, therefore, language does not simply mirror a pre-existing sexist world, but constructs gender asymmetries within specific sociocultural contexts (see Lakoff 1975, Poynton 1989, Motschenbacher 2010). The feminist linguist is then concerned about how people negotiate or construct their gender identities in social practice, either accepting or challenging societal beliefs or ideological constructs through specific ways of using language. Having advocated a critical stance on mainstream novelists' uses of language in terms of gendered identities, this chapter explores the intersection between language and gender identity construction from three discursive directions: marriage and procreation as identity, woman-woman oppression and male-woman subjectivity.

Marriage and procreation as identity

The traditional African philosophy has been that both men and women must be married, for marriage 'is the focus of existence' (Mbiti 1969, 133). Given the remarkably high value placed on marriage and procreation, a member of a community is considered abnormal and a rebel if he or she refuses or fails to marry. Also, if a member of a community is unable to marry at the 'expected time', he or she is taken to have failed both him or herself and his or her community. This is embedded in the communal culture that marriage is a community event: something every member of the community is expected to be involved in for the continuity of humankind. Consequently, as many come of age, they are preoccupied with the thoughts of when and who to marry, if they had none in mind. Besides the fact that marriage is a symbol of maturity, it gives an individual special recognition — identity. People are often recognised and accorded respect as 'full' members of their community because they have fulfilled the expectation of marriage. These traditional African beliefs are replicated in literary situations.

The foregoing implies that many are pressured to marry. It is this societal demand for a woman to be 'complete' through the process of marriage that causes Subu to be pressured by her mother:

> She asks about Subu's mother, who is also widowed (Like Deola's mother) and lives in Lagos.
> 'My mother is well', Subu says. 'Harassing me as usual.'
> 'Still?'
> The pressure to marry is relentless. Being single is like trying to convince a heckling audience your act is worth seeing. Subu could be the chairman of her bank and her mother would say, 'But she could be married with children'. Subu could be the prime minister of England and her mother would still say, 'But she could be married with children'. (Atta 2013, 25)

Perhaps it is unnecessary to mention again that Nigerian literature has continued to give expression to the cultural practices of the Nigerian people. The harassment Subu comes under should probably not be considered unusual, since it resonates with the traditional Nigerian belief that people must marry so that the chain of human continuity will remain unbroken. Hence, Subu's mother's insistence — as captured by the adjective *still* — is not abnormal; rather, it explains the need for every member of a community to play their role in the human continuity axiom. In a similar vein, the conjunctive negator *but* linguistically testifies that an individual's social achievements — be the person a chairman of their bank or the prime minister of England — amount to naught if the person is not married with children. Invariably, from the traditional Nigerian point of view, an achievement such as being the prime minister of England is not considered to worth much if the individual concerned is not married with children. The traditional Nigerian is conscious of this identity marker, that at a certain stage in life they must be married and have children. This is considered the hallmark of life's fulfilment. The implication of Subu's mother's harassment is that an individual's material possessions do not mean much if the individual does not have children who will inherit their parent's wealth. It is this Nigerian custom and belief that informs Subu's mother's persistence that Subu gets married. Subu and Deola work in the UK and since they are considered 'old' enough to be married but are yet to do so, they are already being seen as failures.

Being married and having children have remained important identity markers for many traditional Nigerians. For Odenigbo's mother therefore it is unacceptable and impracticable for her son to stay with a woman who is not capable of having children for him. She neither embellishes her language nor conceals the reason for her visit:

> 'This is why I came. They said she is controlling my son,' Master's mother said, stirring the soup. 'No wonder my son has not married while his mates are counting how many children they have. She has used her witchcraft to hold him.' (Adichie 2007, 125)

If we read Mama's concern vis-à-vis the value some Africans attach to children, it will indicate that she is particularly disturbed by the realisation that Olanna is incapable of making Odenigbo a full man like his 'mates'. But before we forge ahead with our interpretation of Mama's concern, it will be rewarding to survey her linguistic construction. In the first instance, her sentences are short and precise (mostly simple sentences). They depict the urgency of her mission. Where she dissects the enigma of being childless, she brings in a complex sentence — *No wonder my son has not married while his mates are counting how many children they have* —which succinctly details the complexity of the issue at hand: staying with a childless *witch*. It can be argued that her linguistic calibration works perfectly to give expression to her burden. For instance, the verb *hold* means that Olanna has so gripped Odenigbo, psychologically incapacitating him.

As far as Mama is concerned, her son's inability to realise that he is involved in an abnormal relationship, for every normal relationship between a man and a woman must have children, is because he has been bewitched. Inasmuch as one might not agree with Mama, it is important to state that Mama's act is simply an instantiation of the cultural thrust that 'everybody… must get married and bear children… that is the greatest hope and expectation of the individual for himself and of the community for the individual' (Mbiti 1969, 133). In fact, the simple sentence: *This is why I came*, is very exact since it embodies her mission. Therefore, Mama's act clarifies the meaning behind every marriage in some Nigerian communities by pointing out that in a normal union between a man and a woman, such as the one between Olanna and Odenigbo, children must be counted. 'Counting children' is the most important thing Mama is concerned about. Like in the case of Subu, Mama is not concerned about the fact that both parties — Olanna and Odenigbo — are university lecturers: it means nothing to her. It also follows that she has failed to perform her obligation if she idles by and watches her son go childless. The assumption is that Mama's action ought to be appreciated rather than depreciated. Perhaps other women in Mama's situation will support her; they could also do a similar thing since they want their sons to fulfil their manly obligation. It is in the light of this that Mama sends Olanna away and brings in Amala, a woman who has the capacity to bear children. Knowing that Odenigbo will not ordinarily have sex with Amala, Mama made him drink palm wine. And when he is drunk, she also ensures that Amala sleeps with Odenigbo.

Subsequently, Odenigbo and Olanna are pressured by Mama to grasp the necessity for them to perform their community obligation by having a child. After Mama left for the village and they reconciled, Olana and Odenigbo both agree that they have *work* to do:

> 'I won't go today,' she said.
> 'Good. Because we have work to do'.
> She closed her eyes because he was straddling her now… he whispered, 'We will have a brilliant child, a brilliant child,' and she said, 'Yes, yes.' Each time, after he slipped out of her, she pressed her legs together, crossed them at her ankles, and took deep breaths, as if the movement of her lungs would urge conception on. (Adichie 2007, 137)

Needless to say, Olanna, because of her inability to fall pregnant, is an unhappy person. The thought of possible childlessness *dampens her*, makes her sad. The thought that she may not be a mother disturbs her gravely because it is a mark on her identity. Given the community she belongs to, at least from what we have seen so far, it can be gloomy to be without children. The noun *work* dramatises the importance of what having a child means to both Odenigbo and Olanna. They engage in sexual intercourse with the expectation that the sexual meeting will culminate in Olanna's conception. Their refusal to go out because they have *work to do* acutely illuminates the prestige that is placed on children, revealing how 'wasteful' a marriage can be without children. Odenigbo's repetition of *we will have a brilliant child* is quite telling. There is an apt representation of the core traditional Igbo view of the actual essence of sex, even marriage: procreation, not mere companionship. Being married and having children, Mama makes us to understand, give an individual sociocultural recognition. The significance Mama attaches to children makes her question Olanna's identity.

Furthermore, in detailing the essence of their sexual encounter, Odenigbo's choice of the modal verb *will* is both emotional and assuring. It exposes the rationale behind the sexual engagement: not for some pleasure as they used to do but for the purpose of having *a brilliant child*. Interestingly and slightly deviating from Mama's position, the inclusive pronoun *we* implies that both Odenigbo and Olanna are to be simultaneously involved in the procreational process. It also suggests that both are aware that they have a task that needs to be accomplished urgently — to produce *a brilliant child*. This is the reason Olanna *pressed her legs together* and took *deep breaths* so as to complete the conception *work*. She is conscious of the fact that having a child will save her marriage and rescue her from Mama's sneering threats. Moreover, the emphasis is not on just a child, but a *brilliant* one. The inclusion of the adjective — brilliant — means that it is better to have *a brilliant* child than one who is not *brilliant*.

It is this conceptualisation of manhood and womanhood within the framework that an individual must be married to be seen as a man or a woman in the real sense of the word that makes Ivie's mother admonish Deola:

> 'Working, Schooling,' she says, 'at least born *pikin* if you no want to marry. *Wetin*? Your junior sister, Jaiye, has born *pikin*. Your cousin, Ndidi, has born *pikin*. It's you and Ivie we're waiting for now. Let us see our successors before we die. I've told Ivie, 'All this career will get you nowhere as a woman'. (Atta 2013, 126)

Ivie's mother's position is nothing but an enunciation of the traditional Nigerian ideal that the whole kernel of an individual's existence is summed up in the individual's ability to have children. Therefore, she implores Deola to see the need why working and schooling do not mean anything if she is without children. The emphasis is on *pikin*; it recurs four times in her speech (*Pikin* is a Nigerian Pidgin term for a child.) Explicitly stated is the idea that a woman's career is not a prerequisite for her to be identified as a legitimate and acceptable member of her community. This is why Ivie's mother tells Deola, *Make you just hurry up and born pikin* (Make haste and have children). The verb, *hurry*, captures urgency. Deola is thirty-nine years old, and her auntie is afraid that she will not have a child if she does not *hurry* to get one. The inference we draw from Ivie's mother's position is that the woman's identity is expressed by her marital status. This is the reason Deola and Ivie are admonished to at least have children if they do not want to get married. Symbolically, their identity is questioned; it is therefore seen as an offence against one's self and one's community not to be married. Linguistically, the temporal deictic element *−now* — has an underlying expansive meaning. It carries the message that it is Deola's and Ivie's time/turn to demonstrate their womanhood, for Jaiye, Deola's younger sister, and Ndidi, Deola's cousin, have long shown that they are women enough. But then Deola and Ivie, who can be described as 'modern Nigerian women', do not appear to be disturbed that they are getting 'old' and are yet to be married.

Perhaps an interesting aspect of Ivie's mother's characterisation is that she is not known by any name but as Ivie's mother. Since she is nameless, she is identified more as a mother than an 'ordinary' woman. Her 'mother identity' intersects with the role she plays. Her insistence that Ivie and Deola have children out of marriage, if they do not want to be married, does not suggest that she promotes sexual immorality but a demonstration of the expressible worth some people have for children.

It appears that these novelists are telling us that most often in the search for children males are often preferred. Ugwu's sister, Anulika, explains why she wants to have *a baby boy first, because it will place my feet firmly in Onyeka's house* (Adichie 2007, 151). The implication of Anulika's summation is that having a child will not only give her a place in her marital home, but she will be *firmly* established or better placed if the child is male. Consequently, the woman who has male children is better regarded than the one with only female ones. In the traditional Igbo society where *Yellow Sun* has its setting, there is preference for male children because it is believed that the male child is the one who can guarantee the continuity of his line. It can be inferred that a woman will be duly respected if she has a male child. It is this consciousness that informs Anulika's lexical strategy: 'firmly'. Similarly, Mama's rejection of Amala and her Baby is an amplification of what her traditional Igbo community upholds.

Woman-woman oppression

This section of the study examines the role women play in their own subjugation and the suppression of other women. For example, in *Yellow Sun* (Adichie 2007, 124–125) we can see how Mama, through a mechanistic use of language, succeeds in depersonalising a fellow woman, Olanna. How the inability of a marriage to have children is often blamed on the woman was discussed in the previous section. When Mama visits Olanna, Olanna tries to welcome her, but Mama cuts her off. Her language is aggressive: *Do not Mama me*. Mama's use of language reveals that she is unsympathetic to Olanna's plight. Some readers of *Yellow Sun* could find this alarming as their expectation is that Mama, a woman, should ordinarily sympathise with Olanna. But the reverse is the case as Olanna comes under Mama's unembellished vituperation. Her language is coarse in that it is antagonistic to Olanna.

Mama's categorical use of language is worthy of some explanation since it provides a linguistic window into women's devaluation of their own. Her sentential constructions are couched in command and are especially confrontational: *Just leave my son alone* and *tell your fellow witches that you did not find him!* There is also the choice of degrading and disaffiliating expressions: *fellow witches* and *don't mama me*. Mama implies that it is Olanna's comrades, *fellow witches*, who sent her to bewitch her son. *Fellow witches* are also educated women (this is why Mama called Olanna an educated witch), who do not have children, a group Olanna belongs to. Presupposing that Olanna comes from a coven of witches with the intention of bewitching her son, Mama gives Olanna a message to her partners – *Tell your fellow witches you did not find him.* This is a traditional Nigerian way of telling someone that the person's mission has failed. Mama's description of Olanna as *fellow witch* constitutes another layer of linguistic construction of gendered identity. She enacts the idea that some women also see other women as witches. Had it not been so, Mama would not have called a fellow woman a witch.

As the above encounter between Olanna and Mama illustrates, it is Ugwu, a male who intervenes and implores Mama to be lenient and show Olanna compassion. Ugwu's willingness *to gag, to stuff* Mama's mouth with vegetable is to ensure that there is peace in his Master's house and because he likes Olanna. Similarly, his kindness, captured in the directional preposition, *moving towards Olanna*, reveals how much he desires Olanna's happiness and shows her that he is on her side. In yet another example gleaned from *The Cradle*, Catechist, Ungieubua's husband, totally rejects the demeaning way his wife treats Andoukye. In the extract below, Ungieubua is tendentiously involved in devaluing another woman:

> 'See her lies? You will say who did it!' Madam continued, determined not to be stopped by the girl's seeming antics.
> 'Let her alone, first!' Catechist ordered. 'Her swooning testifies that she didn't say anything to anybody!'
> 'Oh you even defend her! Good, go ahead and defend her; you could well have done it — for all I know!'
> 'Ungieubua, you disappoint me.' Catechist said. (Betiang 2011, 21)

Andoukye is pregnant and does not know that her being forcefully 'taken' one harmattan morning by Akomaye, Ungieubua's first son, is the reason for her constant fainting. In her first trimester, for example, she faints and when she comes to, rather than being attended to, she faces Ungieubua's unsympathetic disapprobation. She neither minds Andoukye's state of health nor does she consider the fact that Andoukye is but a girl who knows nothing about being pregnant. It is Catechist, a man, who comes to Andoukye's rescue. Like Ugwu in the example taken from *Yellow Sun*, Catechist's intervention reveals his true identity — the fact that it is morally expedient to show mercy to all, regardless of their gender. Interestingly, Ungieubua's failure in demonstrating concern towards Andoukye becomes the material with which Catechist constructs his positive male identity. Hence, in demonstrating his disappointment in his wife, his language is not cryptic, but very simple and apt — *Ungieubua, you disappoint me.* His intention to make his message succinct and articulable informs his preference for a simple sentence.

However, Catechist's expression of kindness earns him suspicion from his wife: *you could well have done it*. She evidently sees no reason to show an iota of benevolence towards the suffering of another woman — Andoukye. It should be noted that Catechist's disappointment in his wife is not because she accuses him of being responsible for Andoukye's pregnancy, but because he expects that being a woman and a mother, she should understand what a fellow woman is going through as well as offer the needed assistance. Though the content of Andoukye's letter to her unborn son, Unimke, is not made known to Betiang's readers, it can be assumed that she wrote about all that she had suffered, how her pregnancy had come about and Ungieubua's highhandedness. It may not be out of place to conclude that Unimke's hatred for Ungieubua and his total distrust of women (as can be inferred from the way he sleeps with Iyaji and his rape of his auntie, Mary) are all informed by the subjugating treatment his late mother suffered under Ungieubua.

Given this exposé, it can be deduced that some women contribute in one way or another in constructing a negative identity for other women. Before we begin to nurse the idea that both Mama and Ungieubua's verbal castigation of other women is a function of the writers' characterisation, we should not forget that '[c]reative works, irrespective of genre, are derived from the pulse and rhythm of a society' (Odi 2013, 74). Every writer writes in rhythm with the sociocultural consciousness of their time. Suffice it to say that the presentation of Mama and Ungieubua is a reflection or re-creation of what obtains in the writers' respective 'worlds'.

Ungeiubua, like Mama, linguistically devalues Andoukye; she deploys degrading noun phrases such as *lazy animal, Daughter of Satan*, etc. (Betiang 2011, 3) to describe Andoukye. Again, like in the case of Olanna, we are confronted with the issue of the woman being a witch. While Andoukye can be identified as an *illiterate witch* who 'flies' about at night, Olanna is the *educated witch, a literate witch* who simply suffers cynical stereotyping — a wicked and manipulative urban *femme fatale* who luxuriates in the spate of controlling people's sons.

Another angle to Ungieubua's chastisement of Andoukye appears to suggest that even being pregnant does not exempt some women from grave depersonalisation. Similarly, Amala is merely identified for her procreational value and once she 'failed' to produce a male child, she is dumped. She totally vanishes from the author's narrative radar. Never in any part of the narrative is Amala mentioned again. As far as Mama and her society are concerned, Amala is a failure — she failed to produce a male child. Thus, her identity is relegated to the background. In fact, to her community, she is inconsequential.

In another example, this one drawn from Atta's *Difference*, we are shown women's persistence in debasing one another:

> The friction works in her favour. Outside in the corridor, Elizabeth whispers, 'Don't mind her. She is a difficult woman. You know she was a midwife?'
>
> The corridor is empty but for two of them. Deola steps away from the door and keeps her voice low.
>
> 'I know'.
>
> 'I am her in-law. She is well known in the family for being troublesome.'
>
> 'I am just here for a review'. (Atta 2013, 91)

The 'friction' between Deola and Mrs. Nwachukwu (which was highlighted in Chapter 2) offers yet another intriguing perspective to gender identity construction. In this instance, Elizabeth, Mrs. Nwachukwu's assistant, uses the opportunity to vilify her boss. Reading the exchange between Deola and Elizabeth on a surface level, it appears as though Elizabeth's only motive is to expose the supposedly fraudulent engagements of her boss. A close linguistic interrogation, however, reveals that Elizabeth's true aim is to undermine her boss so that she can find favour with LINK, enabling her to finance her own pet project. If Elizabeth were truly concerned about exposing Mrs. Nwachukwu's supposedly dishonest deal, she should have said this in front of Mrs. Nwachukwu, not in a *whisper* and in an *empty* corridor. The noun, *whisper*, is quite compelling; it helps to delineate Elizabeth's authentic identity: a woman who finds pleasure in bringing down other women. And the adjective, *empty*, too is evocative in the way it depicts the hollowness of Elizabeth's existence. Further still, the pronominal choice — *she* — and the persuasive term — *you know* — are both strategic to the motif of the enunciator. These linguistic features calculatingly unfold a scenario of open hate for Mrs. Nwachukwu. Cognisant of Elizabeth's intention, Deola warns: *I'm just here for a review*, not for gossips and prying into people's private life.

It can be said, at least from the preceding illustrations, that the way Mama, Ungieubua and Elizabeth respectively use language is deeply connected with some women's tendency to debase other woman. The 'debasing identity' constructed for Olanna and other women stigmatises them; they are compelled to see themselves as lesser human beings. Having shown that there is woman-woman subjectivity other than the popularly followed view of men constructing a negative identity for women, it is useful to examine another strand of gender identity construction.

Man-woman subjectivity

One aspect of male subjectivity that is represented in the novels is the concept of sexuality. (Sexuality is used in this book in its all-encompassing sense: sex, gender roles, sexual orientation, beauty/handsomeness, eroticism, among others). In many Nigerian communities, as have other world communities, the concept of beauty is 'constructed' by men. In *Yellow Sun*, for instance, Richard tells us how

> Olanna took after their mother, although hers was a more approachable beauty with the softer face and the smiling graciousness and the fleshy, curvy body that filled out her black dress. A body Susan would call *African*. Kainene looked even thinner next to Olanna, almost androgynous, her tight maxi outlining the boyishness of her hips. (Adichie 2007, 80)

Richard's poetic presentation of both Olanna and Kainene instantiates two distinctly interrelated phenomena: first, body sensitivity is a pervasive phenomenon that is articulated in Nigerian literature; second, in constructing 'body identity', language is the most poetic and suitable way of enunciating body image as well as constructing beauty and that which is not beautiful. Suffice it to say that inscription of body image, preferably body identity, in language is a manifestation of society's conscious construction/determination of beauty. Richard informs us that Olanna's well-formed body — fleshy and curvy that filled out her black dress — and her beauty — softer face — is typically African, not European or white. The noun phrase, *approachable beauty*, is very compelling. It suggests that while some beauties are approachable, others are not.

Besides describing Olanna as a prototypical African beauty, Richard's linguistic construction incarnates the idea that for some Africans, the woman must be fleshy, curvy and graciously beautiful for her to be desired by a man. No doubt, Richard's socio-semiotic construction of the African woman is inherently embedded in the traditional characterisation of beauty, for beauty transcends physical looks to include being sexually satisfying.

In terms of gender identity construction, the woman has to be beautiful for her to find a suitor. It was earlier noted how marriage gives the woman social recognition/positive identity in her community. The core of the argument is that the objectification of the woman has the currents and alignments of male dominance. We encounter Ugwu, a young male of thirteen who has already internalised the concept of beauty as it has to do with the traditional Nigerian woman:

> He finally looked at her as she and Master sat down at the table. Her oval face was smooth like an egg, the lush colour of rain-drenched earth, and her eyes were large and slanted and looked like she was not supposed to be walking and talking like everyone else; she should be in a glass case like the one in Master's study, where people could admire her curvy, fleshy body (Adichie 2007, 37)

The above is evidently Ugwu's assertion that beauty is expressed in flesh and curves. Yet, the man does not need to be handsome for him to find himself a bride. And Ugwu laments:

> It had all happened too fast; there had been talk of suitors the last time he visited, but she had spoken of Onyeka in such an indifferent way…Now even

their parents were too swift to talk about Onyeka, his good mechanic job in town, his bicycle, his good behaviour, as if he were already a member of the family. Nobody ever mentioned his stunted height and the pointed teeth that looked like they belonged to a bush rat. (Adichie 2007, 151)

Despite Onyeka's ugliness (as captured in Ugwu's graphic narrative), he still finds himself a beautiful bride in the person of Anulika. The man does not need to be handsome; he only needs to be able to provide for his wife, *to have a good mechanic job in town*. However, this does not suggest that men are entirely exempted from such semiotic construction of handsomeness. Ugwu's photographic presentation of Onyeka's ugliness explains the fact that there is also the traditional Igbo concept of handsomeness: the man has to be tall, muscular and sturdy.

Interestingly, while Olanna's beauty is *African*, Kainene's looks well suit the European concept of beauty, *as Richard admired the lean grace of her arched back. Desire reeled inside him* (Adichie 2007, 374). Obviously, for Richard, Kainene's slim looks agree with his European concept of beauty, the apparent reason he prefers her to Olanna. Needless to say, many young Africans have internalised the European notion of beauty. For instance, Lanre laments how his wife, Eno, *is just getting fatter and fatter* (Atta 2013, 64). It is understandable that one of the reasons Lanre married Eno was because she was slim. Yet, the current trend of events has shown that some young Nigerians are not entirely in favour of slim women. In fact, many young, 'contemporary' Nigerians who were thought to have adopted the European culture of slimness as the model figure of beauty now focus on the Nigerian ideal of the fleshy and curvy body. The ideology of flesh and curve has been reincarnated and rhetoricised in contemporary Nigerian music through wide-ranging metaphors and expressions. The Igbo expression, *ukwu*, which metaphorically means large, curvy hip and its sexual connotation that is used in Timaya's (a popular Nigerian hip-hop artist) songs, simply articulates how many a Nigerian man prefers women with large buttocks to those that are *boyish*. In Chapter 4, attention was drawn to how relevant *ikebe* (large buttocks) is to the Nigerian man. The woman is mostly sexually attractive if she has *ikebe*. And if she wiggles it resourcefully, her chance of attracting men is usually higher than those who have *ikebe* yet are unable to flaunt them. The woman's identity is pragmatically tied to her 'possession' — fleshy buttocks.

It appears that these authors are in their respective works telling us that there is a gender construction where the male is privileged over the female. In most instances, the traditional Nigerian man is privileged to have extramarital sexual encounters. Therefore, the man sees nothing wrong and feels edified that he can have as many women as he desires. For instance, when Odenigbo sleeps with Amala, he is neither condemned by society nor does his conscience prick him. He exonerates himself as he shifts the blame to Mama's palm-wine. He simply makes it clear that the issue should not be taken seriously. Even Ugwu defends his Master. He knows that but for the charm Mama rubbed on Amala's back and the food Mama cooked, nothing would have made his Master sleep with Amala. But when Olanna sleeps with Richard as an act of revenge, she is portrayed as a woman who is morally decadent and uncultured. Even Kainene, whose boyfriend Olanna slept with, reveals how, 'It would be forgivable if it were somebody else. Not my sister' (Adichie 2007, 314).

This implies that Kainene is angry not because Richard slept with a woman but her sister. Aptly articulated is the fact that Richard's sexual affair is only grievous because it was Kainene's sister he slept with. The negator, *not*, constructs the idea that it would have been forgivable if Richard had slept with someone else. The terseness of the expression, *Not my sister*, succinctly depicts the gravity of the offence committed by Richard. Also implied in Kainene's statement is the notion that it is normal for a man to have sexual encounters with other women. Aunty Ifeka also sees it as a normal thing for a man to have extramarital affairs; she says 'Odenigbo has done what all men do and has inserted his penis in the first hole he could find when you were away' (Adichie 2007, 279). Is it appropriate to conclude that Aunty Ifeka and Kainene's summation only helps to entrench as well as normalise men's practice of indulging in extramarital sex? In this way, a superior sexual identity is constructed for men. In fact, in a culture where 'sexual discipline' for women is primarily a basis for moral identity, Olanna's behaviour is totally against the cultural ideal. Izugbara has mentioned that African societies are 'penis-centred[and] male-privileging encourages the ideology of double standard in which males feel morally and physically edified by multiple sexual encounters while women are held as morally and physically tarnished by the same' (2004, 2). While males can have sex with other women, hold conversations about sexual acts and sex organs without restraint, the woman is culturally forbidden to do so. Aboh (2015b) has pointed out that a great deal of the pressure to be silent about sex in Nigeria is steeped in sociocultural values, customs, beliefs and ideologies about what makes good and bad sexual behaviour on the part of the woman. Expressions frequently used to describe sexual desires, parts of the body, sex, among other sexual acts or notions in many Nigerian cultures are often euphemised, directing attention to the cultural silence expected of the woman while dealing with sex-related topics. It is this construction of superior identity for the man over the woman that helps in presenting Olanna as morally weak and also fails to reprimand Odenigbo for sleeping with Amala.

Manliness, better still 'manly identity' is therefore calculated on the capacity of the phallus to have as many women as possible under its erectile power. This appears to be the reason Lanre sees nothing wrong in dating other women as he argues with Deola:

'Why should she trust you when you're texting another woman?'
'What is wrong with that?'
'Nothing, unless you're betraying her.'
'Who's betraying anyone here?'
Deola wriggles her fingers. 'You and your little disappearing acts'.
Lanre used to tell her that men couldn't help but have shows and the sooner she accepted the fact, the less complicated her life would be. (Atta 2013, 122)

Clearly stated, *show* means extramarital sexual activity and Lanre sees it as a normal practice for men to have *shows*. Hidden somewhere in between the seams of Lanre's use of language is the message that he will not confront Funsho if asked to do so for maltreating his sister, Jaiye, for men are allowed to have *shows*. Also depicted in the above fragment is the subjective construction of beauty. Within the broader sociocultural context of Nigeria, body image and personal appearance are very important, particularly to the younger generation. Therefore, we see how Lanre constructs what is normal body weight and that which is abnormal. Lanre goes after other women because Eno, his wife is getting fatter, stigmatising her. Though he uses her weight as an excuse, his extramarital affair — captured in the rhetorical question, *what is wrong with that?* — only authenticates his desire to engage in multiple sexual encounters outside the institution of marriage.

In yet another linguistic construction of gendered identity, Aunty Bisi gives Jaiye this advice before her wedding, 'A woman should be a whore in her bedroom and a whore in her kitchen' (Atta 2013, 120). The expression, *whore*, is imbued with insightful significations in terms of gender identity construction: it connotes the skills a woman needs to be effective in her husband's house. It also signifies that there is nothing wrong for a woman to deploy the sexual skills of a whore with her husband. Therefore, to read the surface meaning of the word is to undermine the deep meaning it is infused with. It means that the woman must do everything to satisfy her man. Aunty Bisi's advice has a fundamental implication: for a woman to be 'marriage material' she must be able to cook good meals and sexually satisfy her husband.

Moreover, Aunty Bisi presupposes that most marriages are not only threatened by a woman's inability to have children, but also the woman's failure to cook good meals. That remediation finds expression in the fact that one of the supposed virtues of a woman is being able to cook well. Aunty Bisi, therefore, imprints in Jaiye's mind the belief that good and tasty meals will make her enjoy her marriage, for no man would want to marry a woman who does not have an interesting relationship with the kitchen. It suffices to say that the identity Aunty Bisi constructs for her children and female relatives is not about finding or understanding themselves; nor is it about getting to realise who they really are in their community. Instead, it is all about finding a man; and knowing how to find their way into their man's heart.

The cultural practice of a woman asserting her marital eligibility through food is also succinctly captured in Atta's *Difference*. When Deola confronts her elder brother, Lanre, for maltreating his wife, Eno, he tells Deola that Eno is getting fatter and does not know how to cook (Atta 2013, 64). More critically, Lanre tells Deola categorically that the reason he goes after other women is because Eno cannot cook. The tone of finality encapsulated in the simple sentence, 'She cannot cook, man', suggests two things: one, he will not stop seeing other women and two, Eno has to improve on her culinary skills for her to find a place in his heart. But Deola considers his reasons banal and asks that they call off the discussion. Deola's strategic deployment of the demonstrative, *this*, clinically captures the banality of Lanre's excesses. In so doing, she disagrees with the idea instantiated by Lanre that everything women do is routine, expected and not worthy of any special commendation.

In drawing this chapter to a close, it is expedient to note that gender discourse should not be glossed over in passing but be meticulously examined, since it is a complex sociocultural reality. Apparently, to assume that a positive identity is constructed for a man and a negative one for a woman, without adequately engaging the text through the prism of context to reveal multiple layers of meanings imbued in the text, could result in the hasty conclusion that a specific linguistic act is either anti-feminist or pro-masculine. The point emphasised in this chapter is that gender identities interweave at multiple layers of subjectivities; the woman can be her own oppressor just as the man can be his own subjugator.

6

Afterword

The central concern of this book is the interconnectedness between language and identity in the Nigerian novel. The core argument is that there is an inseparable bond between the way people use language and the identity they construct, reconstruct or project. In taking an explorative approach to the intersection of Nigeria's social-linguistic situation and the Nigerian novel, this book critically examines how socio-ethnic, multilingual and bilingual situations in Nigeria shape the way writers use language in their creative initiatives. In this way, the book echoes the idea that there is a noticeable reflexivity between the writers' use of language and the Nigerian reality. The postulate of this exercise then is that an investigation of the Nigerian novel, at least from the linguistic perspective, is not just a study of Nigeria's linguistic situation, but an inquiry into how ethnic, national, cultural and gendered identities play major roles in determining writers' use of language. One fundamental aspect of this book lies in its conceptualisation of language as repository of identities: national, ethnic, cultural and gendered. It therefore implies that the use of language transcends stylistic rhetoric because a nuanced analysis of literary works illustrates that Nigerian novelists use language to 'do' many things, such as the enunciation of identities and ideologies.

The methodological use of linguistic and extra-linguistic (sociocultural) tools in the analysis of the sampled texts is considered a valid approach to the study of language and identity in a complex and multilingual society like Nigeria. To rely on linguistic information alone is to implicitly undermine the various dimensions of realities in Nigeria in terms of language use, as well as the underlying ideologies of the selected writers' linguistic preferences. This is premised on the position that literary information alone cannot provide a vivid and elaborate account of the linguistic situation in Nigeria. There is therefore a need for a fusion between extra-textual and literary information.

Having undertaken the kind of analysis this work has, it would be misleading to generalise the findings to other contexts or situations. The fact remains that some of the interpretations that have been made here may vary if placed in a different context. Invariably, context, in its myriad of ways, determines the meaning analysts make from texts. That however does not deter one from exposing certain realities about the use of language in the Nigerian novel. Accordingly, it may be concluded that lexical processes such as loaning, lexical innovations and naming techniques are veritable linguistic resources that Nigerian novelists deploy to construct a Nigerian identity and to describe various forms of identities. These, by and large, expose the intertwined bond of language, identity and literature.

The novelists' adoption and adaptation of indigenous lexical units into English, and the continuous expansion of the meanings of English words, are efforts geared at promoting their indigenous language and culture. In expanding the semantic frontiers of English words, the Nigerian novelists perform two explicit functions: one, they create an international variety of English with a Nigerian identity and, two, they remain locally and internationally intelligible, i.e. their works can be read within and outside the country. It seems fair to conclude that as effective speakers of English, the novelists' intentional use of indigenous expressions, the creation of new words from English and the nativisation or 'Nigerianisation' of English expressions are instances of identity display. While they generally use the standard form of English, in terms of structure and grammar, the inclination to use Nigerian terms/ expressions in place of English must be motivated by reasons that transcend stylo-semantic borders. It then follows that the use of language in the novels is an evidence of 'we-ness': Nigerian-ness. In the study of the social-linguistics of Nigeria's literary English, loaning from indigenous languages is systematically and linguistically striking because it gives relevance to indigenous languages. Therefore, as the novelists continue to use the English language, they personalise or customise English to suit their Nigerian experiences. These customisations are effective in constructing discourses and invariably identities.

In terms of naming, the study shows that in Nigeria, names and naming are unique and special. It is indicated that a name identifies a person as well as provides information about the person's roots. Moreover, names explain the parents' concerns and expectations for the child. Traditional names, then, not only tell us about the attributes the child is expected to acquire, but also about the ethnic beliefs and religious practices of the name giver. In addition, we also saw how names are texts that can be used to 'do' things, for example, differentiate one ethnic or racial group from another. In reading fictionalised characters, it is important to know that writers do not give their characters (particularly major ones) names haphazardly. Each character's name systematically resonates with their identity. It then follows that the use of language, especially in the Nigerian novel, cannot be viewed from the stylistic perspective alone, for words 'say' more than merely beautify an artwork.

This work also shows that the presence of diverse cultures in Nigeria, as well as the overwhelming cultural influence of the West owing to colonialism, Christianity, and later globalisation, can make it difficult to think of a homogenous Nigeria's national identity. That notwithstanding, the use of certain linguistic expressions – Nigerianisms – in Nigerians' deliberate construction of their Nigerian-ness is a clear manifestation of a national Nigerian identity. Thus, Nigerians' acceptance of their diversity supports a multiplicity of identities and it is in the country's multiplicity that we can find implications for an expression of a Nigerian identity and a better understanding of the nuanced nature of identity and its construction in specific situational uses of language.

In conjunction with the views already expressed above, it is necessary to reiterate that despite the multiple languages and subcultures in Nigeria, there are several linguistic items that are used and understood by Nigerians, regardless of the ethnic language in which the word or linguistic expression is rooted. Some of the words or linguistic items have been so 'Nigerianised' that it is quite difficult to tell easily from which ethnic language the linguistic expression is loaned. Even though it is a reality that Nigeria does not have a national language, it is important to restate that the national language (Nigerianism) which we are born into often forms the foundation for the enunciation of our cultural and national identities. It is understandable that language creates considerable differences among people, distinguishing one group from another. In fact, it can establish differences in many different powerful ways. That a Nigerian uses the expression *oya*, a Yoruba expression, distinguishes the Nigerian in a profound way from a non-Nigerian. Some Africans who have watched Nigerian home videos agree that the expression *Na wa oo* (exclamation in Pidgin English) is typically Nigerian. We can conclude that such linguistic expressions can mark off Nigerians from non-Nigerians.

In a far-reaching manner, the sampled novelists' linguistic attitude suggests an attempt to project their ethnic and cultural identities. As noted earlier, they loan words from indigenous languages, not because they want to beautify their work, as it is conceived by stylisticians, but to provide ethno-cultural information about the Nigerian people. This is why even when indigenous words that have English equivalents or can be transliterated into English are often preferred to English ones. We have examined the sampled novelists' use of words that describe cultural practices such as food, music/dance and religious beliefs. By so doing, we have seen how these writers transcend art for art sake to make striking political statements about their origin and about their language. It is in such that we 'see' English words but read indigenous cultural ideas. In this way, the expressions are English, but the thoughts are indigenous.

In terms of gendered identity construction, it has been shown that language is used in different ways to capture the ways both men and women relate in society. There is therefore the need for literary texts to be contextually analysed, so that the many intersecting layers of gendered identities can be duly accounted for. Such a contextualised analysis will enable the critic of the Nigerian novel to see beyond the totalising axiom of male subjectivity to the complex and contradictory trajectories of gendered identities. The conjecture is that an all-round account of gender intersection, rather than leading to closure will open up new interpretive possibilities. It will assist the critic to appreciate the various dimensions in which gender identities are constructed and reconstructed through contextualised language use.

At this juncture it suffices to say that as linguists continue to refine theories and methods for the study of language and its manifestation of identity/ties, one thing needs to be made clear: that identity as an anthropological concept is inconsistent and fragmented hence a singular and direct linguistic method of analysis cannot account for its complex, thorny nature. In fact, the complexity of language-in-use as a resource for the production of social subjectivities is becoming ever more intriguing. Indeed, answers to the dynamic nature of identity must come from new kinds of data, as well as from new kinds of analysis of areas of language hitherto thought to have been exhausted or to have nothing to offer in terms of linguistic, social and cultural meanings. By appreciating the dynamic nature of identity, we are invariably projecting the idea that multiple approaches will guarantee our understanding of how identity is infused, not just in language, but in the 'language' of literature, or, more pertinently, in fictionalised situations.

In all, the blend of critical discourse analysis (CDA), a socio-ethno-linguistic approach and literary discourse analysis has proved to be useful in the interpretation of the multifaceted nature of identity as manifest in the Nigerian novel. This interdisciplinary approach is not only useful in our comprehension of the nexus of language and identity, but also brings about some kind of newness to the analysis of Nigerian literature, for 'interdisciplinarity of this … can synthesize something in a sense entirely new' (Fosl 2016, 3). Moreover, the critical approach to the study of the social nature of language which required this study to transcend the formal linguistic frontiers of language to its social context has revealed how language is bound up with social events. By examining the ordinary meaning of words and their social significations, I have made attempts to resolve the micro/macro level dilemma of critical language analysis. Furthermore, the quantitative angle taken by this study has not only answered the question of subjectivity; it has also helped to strengthen the methods of literary discourse analysis.

Needless to say, the ideological sentiment held by some linguistic purists that literary texts should not be considered veritable data for linguistic analysis seems to have been faulted by the analysis undertaken in this book. A literary work is a composition of linguistic artifacts; hence, it remains an interesting data source for linguists who are interested in the social and cultural meaning of language-in-use.

Moreover, as far as the Nigerian context is concerned, literature and language have always had a particular emotional relationship, making it difficult for Nigerians to gloss over what their writers produce.

Bibliography

Aboh, R. 2012. "Lexical Borrowing as a Resource for the Construction of Identities in Selected 21st-century Nigerian Novels." *Marang: Journal of Language and Literature* 22:51–70.

Aboh, R. 2013a. Lexical and Discursive Construction of Identity in Selected 21st century Nigerian Novels. Unpublished PhD thesis. University of Ibadan.

Aboh, R. 2013b. "Pronominal Strategies: Language and Social Reality in Joe Ushie's Poetry." *University of Uyo Journal of Humanities* 16&17(2): 169–185.

Aboh, R. 2014a. "Beyond Loan Words: Bette-Bendi Ethnic Identity Construction in Liwhu Betiang's B*eneath the Rubble*." *Journal of Pan African Studies* 6 (8): 186–203.

Aboh, R. 2014b. "Neologic Practices: Conflation of Language and Cultural Identity in Nigerian Novels". *Ndunode*: *Calabar Journal of the Humanities*, 11(1): 117–181.

Aboh, R.2015a. "Slang and Multiple Methods of Interpreting Sex and Sexual Identity in the Nigerian Novel." *The African Symposium*15(1): 91–97.

Aboh, R. 2015b. "Slang as Repository of Ingroup and Outgroup Identity Marker in a Catholic Seminary." In *Issues in the Study of Language and Literature: Theory and Practice*, eds. I. Kamalu and I. Tamunobelema, 511–523. Ibadan: Kraft Books.

Aboh, R. 2015c. *Above the Rubble*. Ibadan: Kraft Books.

Achebe, C. 1954. *Things Fall Apart*. London: Heinemann.

Achebe, C. 1964. *Arrow of God*. London: Heinemann.

Achebe, C. 1975. *Morning yet on Creation Day*. New York: Double Day.

Achimbe, E. 2013. "Demystifying the Native-speaker Myth in the new Englishes." In *Language, Literature and Discourse: A Festschrift in Honour of Professor A. 'Lekan Oyeleye*, eds. A. Ogunsiji, A. Kehinde, and A. Odebunmi, 3–22. Ibadan: Stirling-Horden Publishers.

Adebayo, A. 1987. "The Social Functions of the African Novel." *Neohelicon* 14 (2): 297–310.doi:10.1007/BF02094693.

Adejunmobi, M. 1999. "Routes: Language and the Identity of African Literature." *Journal of Modern African Studies* 37 (4): 581–96. doi:10.1017/S0022278X99003146.

Adesanoye, F. 2014. "Of Nigerian English and Nigeria's English." In *English Language Lecture Clinic Series*, ed. A. Akinjobi, 43–62. Ibadan: University of Ibadan.

Adichie, C. 2007. *Half of a Yellow Sun*. Lagos: Farafina.

Aikoriogie, A. M. 2015. "Morphological Creativities and Phrasal Pragmatics in Ngugi wa Thiong'O's *Wizard of the Crow*." *Okike: An African Journal of New Writing* 53:34–48.

Akindele, F. and Adegbite, W. 1999. *The Sociology and Politics of English in Nigeria: An Introduction*. Ife: OAU Press.

Almerico, G. 2014. "Food and Identity: Food Studies, Cultural, and Personal Identity." *Journal of International Business and Cultural Studies* 8:1–7.

Amadi, E. 1966. *The Concubine*. Ibadan and London: Heinemann.

Anderson, B. 1991. *Imagined Communities: Reflections on the Origin and Spread of Nationalism*. London, New York: Verso.

Anyokwu, C. 2011. "Igbo Rhetoric and the New Nigerian Novel: Chimamanda Ngozi Adichie's *Purple Hibiscus*." *The African Symposium* 11(1): 80–90.

Atta, S. 2013. *A Bit of Difference*. Lagos: AAA Press.

Ayeleru, B. 2011. "Linguistic Innovation in the new West -African Europhone Novel: Between Inter-language and Indigenization." *California Linguistic* xxxvi (1): 1–32.

Baker, C. 2001. *Foundations of Bilingual Education and Bilingualism*. New York: Multilingual Matters.

Banjo, A. 1996. *An Overview of the English Language in Nigeria*. Ibadan: Ibadan University Press.

Bandia, P. 1996. "Code-switching and Code-mixing in African Creative Writing: Some Insights for Translation Studies. *TTR: Traduction, Terminologie*." *Rédaction* 9 (1): 139–53.

Bahri, D. 2003. *Native Intelligence: Aesthetics, Politics, and Postcolonial Literature*. Minnesota: University of Minnesota Press.

Bennett, A. 2005. *"Fashion" in Culture and Everyday Life*. London: Sage. doi:10.4135/9781446219256.

Benwell, B. and E. Stokoe. 2006. *Discourse and Identity*. Edinburgh: Edinburgh University Press.

Betiang, L. 2011. *The Cradle on the Scale*. London: Authorhouse.

Birnie-Smith, J. 2015. "Ethnic Identity and Language Choice across Online Forums." *International Journal of Multilingualism* 13(2): 165-183.

Blommaert, J. 2005. *Discourse: A Critical Introduction*. Cambridge: Cambridge University Press. doi:10.1017/CBO9780511610295.

Bradford, R. 1997. *Stylistics*. London: Routledge.

Bodomo, A., and R. Teixeira-E-Silva. 2012. "Language Matters: The Role of Linguistic Identity in the Establishment of the Lusophone African Community in Macau." *African Studies* 71 (2): 37–41.

Bucholtz, M., and K. Hall. 2005. "Identity and Interaction: A Sociocultural Linguistic Approach." *Discourse Studies* 7 (4-5): 585–614. doi:10.1177/1461445605054407.

Butler, J. 1990. *Gender Trouble: Feminism and the Subversion of Identity*. New York: Routledge.

Cameron, D. 2001. *Working with Spoken Discourse*. London: Sage.

Calvet, L. 1997. *Language Wars and Linguistic Politics*. New York: Oxford Press.

Clarke, J. 2005. "Language and the Construction of Identity in Russia." *CERC Working Papers Series* 1: 21–40.

Davies, J. 2004. "Negotiating Femininities Online." *Gender and Education* 16(1): 35-49.

De Fina, A. 2007. "Code-switching and the Construction of Ethnic Identity in a Community of Practice." *Language in Society* 36 (03): 371–92. doi:10.1017/S0047404507070182.

De Cillia, R., M. Reisigl, and R. Wodak. 1999. "The Discursive Construction of National Identities." *Discourse & Society* 10 (2): 149–73. doi:10.1177/0957926599010002002.

Dorais, L. J. 1995. "Language, Culture and Identity: Some Inuit Examples." *Canadian Journal of Native. Studies*. 15 (2): 293–308.

Emmanuel, I. and Aboh, R. 2015. "A Re-assessment of Generationalizations in Nigerian Literature: The Generationalizations Palaver." *Okike: An African Journal of New Writing* 53:136–57.

Eka, D. 2000. *Issues in Nigerian English Usage.* Uyo: Scholars Press (Nig.) Ltd.

Ekwensi, C. 1954. *People of the City.* London: Heinemann.

Eliot, T. S. 1962. "Religion and Literature." In *Five Approaches of Literary criticism.* New York: Macmillan.

Fairclough, N. 1995. *Critical Discourse Analysis: The Critical Study of Language.* London, New York: Longman.

Fairclough, N. 2001. *Language and Power.* 2nd ed. New York: Longman.

Fonchingong, C. 2006. "Unbending Gender Narratives in African Literature." *Journal of International Women's Studies* 8 (1): 135–47.

Fosl, P. 2016. "The Many Voices of Interdisciplinarity." *Cogent Arts & Humanities* 3 (1): 1–9.doi:10.1080/23311983.2016.1164949.

Fowler, R. 1981. *Literature as Social Discourse: The Practice of Linguistic Criticism.* Bloomington: Indiana University Press.

Fowler, R. 1996. *Language in the News: Discourse and Ideology in the Press.* London: Routledge.

Gee, P. 2005. *An Introduction to Discourse Analysis: Theory and Method.* London: Routledge.

Griswold, W. 2000. *Bearing Witness: Readers, Writers, and the Novel in Nigeria.* Princeton: Princeton University Press.

Hall, S. 1994. *Rassismus und Kulturelle Identität. Ausgewählte Schriften 2.* Hamburg: Argument Sonderband.).

Hagstrom, C. 2012. "Naming Me, Naming You. Personal Names, Online Signatures and Cultural Meaning." *Oslo Studies in Language* 4 (2): 81–93.

Halliday, MAK. 1970. Language Structure and Function. In *New Horizons in Linguistics,* ed. J. Lyons, 140–165. Harmondsworth: Penguin.

Hristova, T. 2014. "Clothing–A Choice and Image of Cultural Identity." *Postmodernism Problems* 4 (1): 80–87.

Ibukun, F. and Omotosho, M. 2014. "A Socio-semiotic Study of Nicknaming among Undergraduates in a Nigerian University." *Linguistik Online* 68 (6): 21–42.

Isingoma, B. 2014. "*Empaako* 'Praise Names': An Historical, Sociolinguistic, and Pragmatic Analysis." *African Study Monographs* 35 (2): 85–98.

Izugbara, C. O. 2004. "Patriarchal Ideology and Discourses of Sexuality in Nigeria." Understanding Human Sexuality Seminar Series 2. 1-34. Africa Regional Sexuality Resource Centre, Lagos, Nigeria.

Jack, D. 1991. *Silencing the Self: Women and Depression.* Cambridge: Harvard University Press.

Jaspal, R. 2009. "Language and Social Identity: A Psychological Approach." *Psychtalk* 64: 17-20.

Jaspal, R. 2012. "The Construction of Ethnic Identity: Insights from Identity Process Theory." *Ethnicities* 12(5): 503-530.

Johnstone, B. 2008. *Discourse Analysis.* 2nd ed. Oxford: Blackwell Publishing.

Joseph, J. E. 2004. *Language and Identity: National, Ethnic and Religious.* New York: Palgrave. doi:10.1057/9780230503427.

Jowitt, D. 1991. *Nigerian English Usage.* Lagos: Longman.

Jowitt, D. 1995. "Nigeria's National Language Question: Choices and Constraints." In *New Englishes – A West African Perspective,* eds. A. Bamgbose, A. Banjo and A. Thomas, 31–47 Ibadan: Mosuro Publishers.

Jowitt, D. 2014. "Nigerian English Usage: Neologisms and Archaisms." In English *Language Lecture Clinic Series*, ed. A. Akinjobi, 63–82. Ibadan: University of Ibadan.

Kavalski, E. 2003. "Notions of Voluntary Identity and Citizenship in the *Wonderful Adventures of Mrs. Seacole in Many Lands. Jouvert: A Journal of Postcolonial Studies* 7(2): 1-12.

Kroskrity, P. V. 1999. "Identity." *Journal of Linguistic Anthropology* 9(1-2): 111–14. doi:10.1525/jlin.1999.9.1-2.111.

Ladele, O. 2009. "Reconstructing Identities through Resistance in Postcolonial Women's Writing: A Reading of Ezeigbo's *The Last of the Strong Ones*." *Nebula* 6 (3): 70–84.

Lakoff, G. 1975. *Language and Women's Place.* New York: Harper and Row.

Le Page, R., and Tabourate-Keller, A. 1985. *Acts of Identity: Creole-based Approaches to Language and Ethnicity.* Cambridge: Cambridge University Press.

Le Page, R. 1986. "Acts of Identity." *English Today* 1 2(4): 21–24. doi:10.1017/S0266078400002418.

Maingueneau, D. 2010. "Literature and Discourse Analysis." *Acta Linguistica Hafniensia* 42:147–58.

Mayr A. 2004. *Prison Discourse: Language as a Means of Control and Resistance.* London: Palgrave Macmillan.

Mbiti, J. 1969. *African Religions and Philosophy.* London: Heinemann.

McGregor, S.L.T. 2003. "Critical Discourse Analysis- A Primer." *Kappa Omicron Nu FORUM* 15 (1). Accessed August 13, 2015, https://www.kon.org/archives/forum/15-1/mcgregorcda.html

Mbakogu, I. 2002. "Socio-cultural Factors and Ethnic Group Relationships in Contemporary Nigerian Society." *African Anthropologist* 9 (2): 117–36.

Mills, S. 1995. *Feminists Stylistics.* New York: Routledge.

Montanari, M. 2004. *Food is Culture.* Columbia: Columbia University Press.

Motschenbacher, H. 2010. *Language, Gender and Sexual Identity: Postculturalist Perspectives.* Amsterdam, Philadelphia: John Benjamins Publishing. doi:10.1075/impact.29.

Ndibe, O. 2000. *Arrows of Rain.* Oxford: Heinemann Educational Books.

Ngugi, wa T. 1997. *Writers in Politics: A Re-engagement with Issues of Literature and Society.* Oxford: James Currey.

Nwafor, O. 2013. "The Fabric of Friendship: *Aso ebi* and the Moral Economy of Amity in Nigeria." *African Studies* 72 (1): 1–18. doi:10.1080/00020184.2013.776195.

Odi, C. 2013. "Concept of Witchcraft in African Drama and Negative Female Stereotyping in Select Nigerian Plays." *Wilberforce Island Review* 11:71–82.

Okereke, G. 2014. "African Feminist Dialogics: Gender and Multi-dimensional Politics in Selected African Novels." *Currents in African Literature and the English Language* 9:19–36.

Okunrinmeta, U. 2013. "Bilingualism and Linguistic Influence in Nigeria: Examples from the Works of Achebe and Emecheta." *International Journal of English Linguistics* 3 (4): 117–28. doi:10.5539/ijel.v3n4p117.

Olaoye, A. 2013. "Nigerian Dress Culture: A Linguistic and Anthropological Communication Tool." *Journal of ELT and Applied Linguistics* 1 (2): 32–42.

Omi, M. and Winant, H. 1994. *Racial Formation in the United States* 2nd ed. New York: Routledge.

Omoniyi, T. and White, G. ed. 2006. *The Sociolinguistics of Identity*. London, New York: Continuum.

Onwueke, A. I. 2009. "The Socio-cultural Implications of African Music and Dance." *Creative Artist: A Journal of Theatre and Media Studies* 3(1): 117-185.

Ononye, F. and Aboh, R. 2010. "Slang in Text Messaging amongst Nigerian University Students." In *Studies in Slang and Slogans*, eds. S. Babatunde, A. Odebunmi, A. Adetunji and M. Adedimeji, 165–184. Muenchen: LINCOM.

Orchardson-Mazrui, E. 2006. "The Impact of Cultural Perceptions on Gender Issues." In *Gender Inequalities in Kenya*, eds. C. Creigton and F. Yieke, 144–165. UNESCO.

Osundare, N. 2012. "Our Perception of African Literature Should Be Endogenous." In *Nigerian Literature: The 21ˢᵗ Century Conversation*, ed. O. Ezechi, 182–217. Ibadan: Kraft Books.

Oyeleye, L. 1991. "*Things Fall Apart* Revisited: A Semantic and Stylistic Study of Characters in Achebe." *African Literature Today* 17:18–32.

Paltridge, B. 2006. *Discourse Analysis*. London, New York: Continuum.

Porras, J. E. 2011. "'Black Spanish' Speech as Ethnic Identity in Afro-Colombian Poetry: The Case of Candelario Obeso." *Journal of Pan African Studies* 4 (5): 262–86.

Poynton, C. 1989. *Language and Gender: Making the Difference*. Oxford: Oxford University Press.

Salman, S. A. 2013. "Language and Style in Okot p'Bitek's 'Song of Ocol'." In *Language, Literature and Discourse: A Festschrift in Honour of Professor A. 'Lekan Oyeleye*, eds. A. Ogunsiji, A. Kehinde, and A. Odebunmi, 113–124. Ibadan: Stirling-Horden Publishers.

Short, M. 1998. *Exploring the Language of Poems, Plays and Prose*. London, New York: Longman.

Simpson, P. 1993. *Language, Ideology and Point of View*. New York: Routledge. doi:10.4324/9780203312612.

Simpson, P. 2014. *Stylistics*. New York: Routledge.

Simpson, P. and Mayr, A. 2010. *Language and Power: A Resource Book for Students*. London: Routledge.

Soyinka, W. 1988. *Art, Dialogue and Outrage*. Ibadan: New Horn Press.

Soyinka, W. 1975. *Death and the King's Horseman*. London: Eyre Methuen.

Soyinka, W. 1965. *The Interpreters*. London: Heinemann.

Suleiman, Y. 2006. "Constructing Language, Constructing National Identities." In *The Sociolinguistics of Identity*, eds. T. Omoniyi and G. White, 50–74. London, New York: Continuum.

The Oxford Companion to the English Language. Oxford: Oxford University Press.

Thornborrow, J. and S. Wareing. 1998. *Patterns in Language: An Introduction to Language and Literary Style*. London: Routledge.

Tunca, D. 2014. *Stylistic Approaches to Nigerian Fiction*. London: PalgraveMacmillan. doi:10.1057/9781137264411.

Twigg, J. 2009. "Clothing, Identity and the Embodiment of Age." In *Aging Identity: A Postmodern Dialogue,* eds. J. Powell and T. Gilbert, 93–104. New York: Nova Science Publishers.

UNESCO 2009. UNESCO World Report 2: Investing in Cultural Diversity and Intercultural Dialogue. UNESCO Publishing.

Ushie, J. and D. Imbua. 2011. *Essays on the History, Language and Culture of Bendi*. Ibadan: Kraft Books.

Ushie, J. and Aboh, R. 2013. "'Igbo Linguistic Expressions' as Ethnic Identity in Elechi Amadi's *The Concubine*." *International Journal of English Language and Literature* 2 (1-2): 39–53.

Ushie, J. and Aboh, R. 2014. "Lexical Innovations in Nigerian Novels: A Critical Discourse Investigation." *Okike: A Journal of New African Writing* 51: 126–146.

van Dijk, T. 2001. "Multidisciplinary CDA: A Plea for Diversity." In *Methods of Critical Discourse Analysis*, eds. R. Wodak and M. Meyer, 95–120. London: Sage Publications.

Verdonk, P. 2002. *Stylistics*. Oxford: Oxford University Press.

Weiss, G. and Wodak, R. 2003. *Critical Discourse Analysis: Theory and Interdisciplinarity*. Basingstoke: Palgrave Macmillan.

Widdowson, H. G. 1975. *Stylistics and the Teaching of Literature*. London: Longman Publishing.

Windt-Val, B. 2012. "Personal Names and Identity in Literary Contexts." *Names and Identity, Osla Studies in Language* 4 (2): 273–84.

Wodak, R. 2006. "Critical Linguistics and Critical Discourse Analysis". *Handbook of Pragmatics* 10: 1–25. doi:10.1075/hop.10.cri1.

Wodak, R. 2010. "Critical Discourse Analysis: Some Important Concepts and Considerations." Accessed March 20, 2012 at http://www.long.lancsac.uk.profiles/Rutt-Wodak/

Yahya, Z. 2003. *Resisting Colonialist Discourse*. Bangi: UKM.

Index

Page numbers in *italics* refer to tables.

Index